Table of Contents

Acknowledgments

I want to thank my lovely wife, Nancy, for her patience in allowing me to spend countless Saturday afternoons and Sundays on this book. I also want to thank my editors Andrés Rodríguez, Rita Arens, and Toni Sciarra Poynter for their skill and persistence. My longtime friend and colleague, Charles L. Sheridan, Ph.D., deserves special thanks for his many comments and contributions. I'm most grateful to the clients who shared their feelings and entrusted themselves and their confidence to me. I owe Bernard and Martha Sullivan, my parents, too much to mention.

Kate is a composite of several clients, but all other clients in this book are real people whose names and identifying characteristics have been changed to protect their privacy. I thank them for letting me describe their situations in the interest of helping others.

I began seeking stronger self-confidence at age 14. As a psychologist, I found all available confidence building techniques failed me, my clients, and many of my colleagues, so I developed Core Confidence Theory and Confidence Release Technique in the latter half of my 34 years of practice. My clients' exciting progress made me want to offer this technique to the public.

I wrote this book, using simple concepts, to help the millions of people who desperately want the confidence to feel comfortable in their own skins. The science behind evolutionary psychology is still emerging. Neuroscience is controversial and stupefyingly complex. I did not write this book to further those fields. Rather, I do my best to describe some brain functions in general, simple, and sometimes symbolic terms only for the purpose of making Core Confidence Theory more easily understandable.

CHAPTER 1

Your Biological Belief in Yourself

"Our deepest fear is not that we are inadequate. Our deepest fear is that we are powerful beyond measure."

— MARIANNE WILLIAMSON

Confidence has fascinated me ever since the sixth grade when I struggled to work up the nerve to kiss my first girlfriend. She was comfortable and ready to be kissed—I was all butterflies, dry mouth, and knotted muscles. Back in those Dark Ages, long before the dawn of feminism, men were supposed to have the magnificent poise that carried movie heroes through crises and swept women off their feet. I wasn't supposed to have less confidence than a sixth grade girl.

I wanted Charles Lindbergh's astonishing confidence. I remember watching grainy movies of his tiny, single-engine plane slogging down a rain-drenched runway, barely clearing the power lines at the end, and rising into an ominous sky. Two-man teams of famous pilots flying tri-engine planes designed by geniuses had failed to cross the Atlantic, and six had died trying. What magic feeling could inspire an unknown, 25-five-year-old college dropout to believe he could fly off the shores of New York, alone, and for thirty-three hours soar over 3,000 miles of dark, cold ocean? I couldn't even convince myself to feel calm taking math tests, and I remained so nervous around girls that I couldn't think of anything to say that didn't sound stupid.

In general, my confidence was never less than average. It's just that average confidence is awful. You doubt your decisions, criticize yourself, worry about performance reviews, or shrink from speaking in public. You certainly don't get to relish rising to meet your daily challenges fully believing in yourself and doing your best.

I hit puberty early. Between sixth and tenth grades, I was the strongest, fastest, and best hitter on the baseball team. So why did I go to the plate worrying about striking out, with my palms so wet that when I swung hard, sometimes the bat flew out of my hands and whirled down the third base line, coaches and players diving for cover? Trying to look calm and cool, I told myself to relax, that it was silly to be nervous. I thought a real man would step up to the plate smiling, hungry for a home run, and, like the great Roger Hornsby, feeling sorry for the pitcher.

What did that mysterious confidence really feel like? My dad said that confidence kept you from clutching under pressure, that it let you relax, concentrate, and bring all your strength and talent to bear on the task before you. I had heard people say, "I knew I could do it" or "I trusted myself." I had no idea what believing in myself felt like or how to do it.

Years later, NBA superstar Michael Jordan best described the feeling I wanted in his video documentary *Come Fly with Me*: "If I get the ball, you're at the mercy of whatever I want to do, and there is nothing you can say or do about it. The feeling is I own the ball, I own the game, I own the guy who's guarding me. I can actually play him like a puppet." Even on last-second, win-or-lose shots, Jordan didn't doubt himself, saying, "Whenever we need it, I always believe I can do it," and "God destined me to make this shot."

I didn't know that such a sense of worth, strength, and importance could effortlessly ignite a rousing feeling of "Yes, I can" and pump excitement and eagerness through your body. I didn't know that confidence made you feel stronger, smarter, faster, bigger, and better. I had no idea that it let you see yourself vanquishing your competition. I never thought I could expect to vanquish. What was the difference between nervous me and Michael Jordan?

By eighth grade I was fed up and swore that low self-confidence would not ruin my life. I have now been at war with it for 50 years. I began with self-help books, which claimed that believing in yourself showed in your body language and made others believe in you and want to hang out with you, date you, or hire you. They also claimed that your confidence was contagious and could inspire your teammates and co-workers. For my purposes, it seemed like the secret to acing tests, getting girls, and hitting home runs. I hoped to escape my tense, mediocre existence and stride through life feeling powerful, successful, and happy. So I did what the books said. For example, I reminded myself that even if I struck out I was still OK.

The books didn't help much. My hands were still sweaty and self-doubt still plagued me. I wondered: *If being the best and reading self-confidence books don't help, what the heck is wrong with me? Am I just not made of the right stuff?* Lacking confidence, I felt as though I was failing a little every day.

As a college freshman, I hoped to earn confidence by winning a Golden Gloves boxing tournament. I studied a book on boxing and trained for months. I knew that a true champion would believe in himself, but I didn't know how to get myself to climb into the ring—eager, feeling invincible, and totally engaged, ready to use every ounce of strength and talent in a rip-roaring experience that dwarfed winning or losing. The tournament week should have been a thrilling memory, one to savor until old age. Instead I was tense and worried every waking moment, obsessively planning strategies and memorizing combinations of punches. In the championship match, my ever-present self-doubt made me feel that I'd already lost as I was fighting the final round.

I won that match. So why did I fight the final round feeling I had lost? And though I enjoyed the recognition and newspaper clippings that followed, why did none of it make me feel more confident? What caused my relentless self-doubt? Years later, when earning a doctorate in psychology didn't yield more confidence, I began to doubt that successes or external methods could build it. Yet I persisted with self-help programs. I even dreamed up the country's first psychology/self-improvement store, The Creative Mind, and opened it with my wife, Nancy, in 1986. We stocked thousands of books, tapes, and videos, expanding eventually to two stores and two franchises. Yet after roughly 15,000 client sessions in more than fifteen years in private practice, I, like many of my colleagues, still couldn't figure out how to help clients find true confidence. It seemed that true confidence must be more than traditional psychology theory said it was.

Traditional Confidence Theory Doesn't Deliver

Many years of studying both academic and self-help literature showed me that most confidence-building books and programs follow a traditional theory. They claim that we absorb our failures and mistakes into our basic self-concept alongside the criticism, rejection, neglect, or other mistreatment we receive during childhood. Consequently, our rickety but fundamental sense of self is (supposedly) riddled with feelings of inadequacy, insecurity, and self-doubt.

To gain confidence, the theory goes, we must heal our damaged selves by throwing out self-critical beliefs such as "I'm not smart enough." Next we're supposed to program in new, positive beliefs about our worth such as "I'm love-able." Sound familiar?

Unfortunately, traditional confidence-building techniques, such as affir-mations and positive thinking spawned by this theory deliver little more than spoonfuls of confidence. Psychologists Joanne Wood, Elaine Perunovic, and John Lee recently published research showing that affirmations attempting to make people with low self-esteem think more positively about themselves had the opposite effect: "When people with low self-esteem repeated the statement, *I'm a lovable person*, or focused on ways in which the statement was true of them, neither their feelings about themselves nor their moods improved—they got worse." Positive self statements provided only a small improvement to people whose self-esteem was already high. The researchers proposed that if people with low self-esteem don't believe the positive self statement "I am lovable," then their failure to meet that standard makes them feel worse about themselves.

That had certainly been my experience whenever I attempted to bolster my self-esteem with positive self-talk. In high school I tried to sell cutlery door-to-door. I read self-help books in my car outside potential customers' houses to stimulate an "I-can-do-this" feeling, but by the time I knocked on their doors, my palms were sweating again. In my experience, self-help books only make you feel better about yourself while you're reading the book.

Even successful achievement doesn't seem strongly related to confidence, as I learned after winning that boxing match. I know people with little talent or success who feel great about themselves. Furthermore, people who have endured many failures, heavy criticism, and other negative experiences often have great confidence.

Throughout his life, Winston Churchill possessed enormous confidence, despite many failures and severe neglect from his parents. His father criticized him harshly as a boy, usually treating him with thinly veiled hostility. (Churchill did have a devoted nanny. But—if traditional theories were correct about failures and childhood wounds causing low confidence—it seems unlikely that her affection would have overcome the negative effect of the persistent and pervasive failures, criticism, and neglect that he endured.) In school, Churchill failed so miserably that, despite his father's powerful status as a politician and the son of the Duke of Marlborough, he couldn't get into college. Churchill had to attend army cadet school, where he learned about guns and horses.

Despite all of this neglect, criticism, and failure, Churchill radiated confidence. At 17, he told a schoolmate that one day England would be engaged in a terrible war. "I shall be in command of the defenses of London and England," he said, "It will fall to me to save the Capital and the Empire." At 24, lacking any college education, he felt qualified to run for Parliament.

In 1939, after Germany had crushed the French and British armies, the French generals told their prime minister that if England didn't ask for peace, Germany would wring its neck like a chicken. Most of the world agreed, including the majority of the politicians in Britain and the United States. But core confidence made 70-year-old Winston Churchill believe that Great Britain could stand alone against the might of the German war machine, and that he would lead them to victory.

His confidence and stirring speeches inspired England to fight on, loss after terrible loss. Had England not hung on for two years until the attack on Pearl Harbor brought the United States into the war, the Nazis would likely have won the war and controlled Europe, Russia, North Africa, and the Middle East.

Churchill's undaunted confidence, unexplainable by the traditional theory of self-confidence, shows the strength of our deepest belief in ourselves. One of my favorite Churchill quotes is "We are all worms. But I do believe that I am a glow-worm."

Unlike Churchill's upbringing, mine provided no excuse for my lack of confidence. My parents weren't rejecting or unusually critical. They were kind and supportive, and I was able to get a solid education. This left me totally responsible for my self-doubts. Based on my own experience, decades of reading on the topic, and training as a psychologist, I think that traditional self-confidence theory recommendations, such as setting goals and thinking positively, produce so little confidence that most of us yearn for more. We want unshakable confidence.

Piecing Together the Inborn Confidence Puzzle

In the 1980s, an intriguing new field called evolutionary psychology illuminated how evolution influences personality and behavior. It states that pecking orders or social hierarchies drive most species to improve and survive, ensuring that the strongest, healthiest alpha male and female struggle to the top and mate with each other to produce stronger offspring. Internationally renowned primatologist Frans de Waal, summarizing this widely accepted theory in his fascinating book, *Our Inner Ape,* wrote, "We are born to strive for status." He described the lives of primates, our closest animal relatives, as permeated by their ever-present awareness of their social hierarchy. He shows how powerfully and pervasively we are influenced by our human desire to be at the top of the social hierarchy. For example, he described numerous arguments between academic scientists that – when fueled by the pecking order desire to be right or dominant – left the rationality of science and descended into emotional barbarism.

Two eminent anthropologists, Robert Trivers, Ph.D., at Rutgers and Richard Wrangham, Ph.D., at Harvard, each published scientific articles theorizing about high self-confidence enhancing our ancestors' survival success in conflicts and competitive settings. Wrangham hypothesized that "positive illusions" (think high confidence) increase survival for two main reasons. First, they enhance personal performance by "reducing stress and negative thoughts and feelings . . . in sports terminology, positive illusions enable 'championship thinking' or 'psyching up.'" Second, positive illusions help us bluff or deceive our opponents in contests or military conflicts, because if we really believe that our own superiority will ensure our success, our body language radiates our certainty about our superiority and we are the most intimidating to our opponents. Wrangham writes: "In conflicts involving mutual assessment, an exaggerated assessment of the probability of winning increases the probability of winning . . . Selection therefore favors this form of overconfidence."

On this second point, Wrangham quotes Trivers, who has developed an extensive theory of self-deception as an evolutionary survival enhancing trait. Unconsciously deceiving ourselves with positive illusions about our strengths or abilities increases confidence. Part of Trivers's fascinating theory hypothesizes that positive illusions are effective in helping us successfully bluff (or intimidate) our opponents in contests or conflicts because they lessen "behavioral leakage," body language that gives our bluff away. Trivers cites impressive scientific studies suggesting that positive illusions prevent three types of behavioral cues or body language from giving our bluff away. These three revealing behavioral cues are

- Nervousness,
- The effort to hide or control nervousness, and
- The time and concentration (cognitive load) required to lie or pretend effectively.

Surprisingly, Trivers shows that the cognitive load is by far the most revealing cue.

In 1994 Robert Wright, an award-winning science writer, published a fascinating book, *The Moral Animal,* that reviews many of the theories and supporting evidence in evolutionary psychology. Wright integrates theories and research on self-deception and positive illusion and their likely substantial contribution to achieving higher social status in pecking orders. He makes a persuasive argument that self-deception and positive illusion helped our ancestors survive. Imagine the confidence it took to face a woolly mammoth with a sharpened stick. An unflagging belief in themselves probably helped our ancestors to face withering famines, failed hunts, and marauding predators. They passed that confidence on to us.

Does this mean that confidence is inborn? It seems so. And because we inherited the same primitive emotional system that enabled our ancestors to meet enormous challenges, our own tests and trials should similarly stimulate confidence inside us.

I began to wonder about the physical *experience* of pecking order emotion. What feeling drove our ancestors to claw, bite, or snarl their way to the top? Did it surge inside them? Was it an "I-should-be-at-the-top-I-should-have-the-strongest-and-healthiest-mates-I-will-sleep-by-the-fire-you-move-over" directive? I wondered: Does human self-confidence today flow from an inborn ability to experience sensuous, spine-tingling, heart-pounding, chest-thumping, physical confidence—the same confidence that caused our ancestors to feel that they were smarter, stronger, faster, and entitled to the biggest portion of the kill and the warmest part of the cave?

I believe that we do have this wellspring of instinctive self-confidence, but that most of us unconsciously suppress it. Research indicates that when we talk to someone our emotional brain is assessing who has the highest status in the pecking order and adjusts our body language accordingly often without our awareness. For example, primatologist Frans de Waal described the results of two social psychology studies by S. W. Gregory, T. J. Gallagher, and S. Webster. These studies showed that every time we talk with someone (whether in person or on the telephone) the individual of higher status unconsciously exudes body language that demonstrates their superior status and that lower status individuals unconsciously express body language denoting deference to the higher status individual. De Wall wrote:

> Scientists used to consider the frequency band of 500 Hz and below in the human voice as meaningless noise, because when a voice is filtered, removing all higher frequencies, one hears nothing but a low pitched hum. All words are lost. Then it was found that this low hum is an unconscious social instrument. It is different for each person, but in the course of a conversation, people tend to converge. They settle on a single hum, and it is always the lower status person who does the adjusting. This was first demonstrated in an analysis of the *Larry King Live* television show. The host, Larry King, would adjust his timber to that of high-ranking guests, like Mike Wallace or Elizabeth Taylor. Low ranking guests, on the other hand would adjust their timber to that of King.
>
> The same spectral analysis has been applied to televised debates between U.S. presidential candidates. In all eight elections between 1960 and 2000 the popular vote matched the voice analysis: the majority of people voted for the candidate who held his own timber rather than the one who adjusted.

De Waal also noted that we create visible, touchable symbols and behaviors that show our status, "we have ways of making the human hierarchy explicit, from the size of our offices to the price of the clothes we wear.... In Japan, the depth of the greeting bow signals precise rank differences not only between men and women (with women bowing more deeply), but also between senior and junior family members."

Recent research shows that our brain instinctively produces what psychologist and neuroscientist Tali Sharot, Ph.D. calls our "biological bias toward optimism." This inborn optimism helped our ancestors survive. Dr. Sharot is a research fellow at the Wellcome Trust Centre for Neuroimaging at University College London. She states that we are biologically wired to "overestimate the likelihood of encountering positive events in the future and to underestimate the likelihood of experiencing negative events." Her fascinating book *The Optimism Bias* (2011) presents cognitive science research showing that, whether we are young or old, our brains instinctively generate feelings of hope and optimism and that "most people maintain an often irrationally positive outlook on life... In fact, although most of us are unaware of it, our inborn optimism may be crucial to our existence." Sharot states that data clearly shows that most people overestimate their prospects for professional achievement. They expect their children to be extraordinarily gifted, and they miscalculate their likely lifespan (sometimes by 20 years or more). They expect to be healthier than the average person and more successful than their peers. They hugely underestimate their likelihood of divorce, cancer, and unemployment. And they are confident over all that their future lives will be better than those their parents put up with.

Although hope and optimism are not the same feeling as self-confidence, the fact that this research clearly shows that our brain is biologically encoded to generate primitive positive feelings strongly supports the idea that something as important to survival as confidence would also be biologically encoded.

I believe that instinctive self-confidence also benefitted our ancestors in many areas besides competition and conflict. For example, I suspect that believing they were strong and smart enough to find food, build a hut, make an arrow fly straighter, or invent a better cutting instrument increased the chances that their descendants would do so too. I believe that in our world today, the belief in ourselves that helps us to fly the Atlantic, make the basket, sink the putt, save the country, give a speech or sales presentation, or ask for a date, raise, or promotion all flow from instinctive confidence.

This book seeks to help you uncover the pervasive, powerful ability within you so that you can relish it and harness its strength, passion, and energy.

Just Because You Can't See It Doesn't Mean It Isn't There

Most people can't consciously feel core confidence and therefore doubt that it's there and that anything could help them feel it. In the middle of World War II, my dad turned 17, enlisted in the Navy, and graduated from Notre Dame's midshipmen school as an ensign. He had so much confidence that he volunteered to be a naval gunfire reconnaissance officer. That meant swimming at night from a mostly submerged submarine onto a Japanese-held island to radio back to the armada information about where their shells were falling. He said, "Fortunately, the Navy sent me to anti-aircraft officer school." On the first day he was sitting in a classroom with about 30 other ensigns. Every few seconds a small slide projector was flashing a 10 ft. white image on the front wall for a tiny fraction of a second.

After 10 minutes a middle-aged officer came in and asked if the plane that was partially hidden in the clouds of the image was American, German, or Japanese. My dad, a friendly, witty Irishman and just a little cocky, said, "Sir, I can't even make out the clouds." The officer replied, "Keep looking. On a cloudy day if you can't see them 5 miles out for the tenth of a second as they come out of one cloud and disappear into the next, they'll be on you before you can get your gun crew firing."

The officer temporarily lengthened the flash to half a second and soon everyone was able to identify the clouds. By the end of the day everyone could see the tiny image of the plane between the clouds. After a few days of persisting at looking, everyone was able to tell whether the plane was American, German, or Japanese.

Even if you can't see something, it can still be there.

Studies show that if they had been flashing an emotionally charged image such as a beautiful woman, the sailor's emotional brains would've responded unconsciously before they had any conscious awareness of the image. Similarly, we all have feelings that we can't experience consciously, and they powerfully influence our choices, decisions, and actions. Even if you consciously feel that you don't possess any core confidence, I'm going to brighten the light, lengthen the flash, and show you where to look. If you persist and keep looking, you may get a glimpse of your core confidence.

Logic and Facts Don't Build Solid Confidence

Recognizing the biological nature of confidence helped me to understand why traditional approaches failed to build solid confidence. For years I had been trying to replace negative thoughts about myself with positive ones. I repeated affirmations such as "You're talented and lovable." Sometimes they helped me feel a little better, but the feeling was temporary, and ultimately I found these superficial aids to be about as sturdy as a house of cards.

I began to wonder if brain structure and function might explain the shortcomings of affirmations. During my first two years in graduate school, I primarily studied neuropsychology. During that time, I learned that our thinking brain systems are largely separate from our feeling brain systems. It's possible that traditional confidence-building approaches have little success because the facts in our thinking brains, such as "I'm a champion" or "I'm a doctor," don't reach our primitive feeling system.

The brain is divided into two parts. The much older, primordial feeling part generates core emotions that energize basic survival behavior. The thinking part evolved only about 100,000 years ago because it helped us plan and solve complex problems. These separate brain systems are symbolically shown in Figure 1.

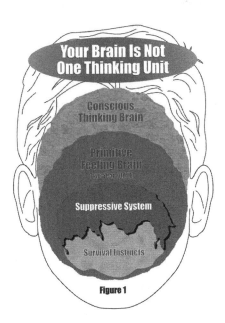

Figure 1

These parts are neither well connected physically nor on the same level rationally, so they have limited communication and understanding of each other. Crudely speaking, the brain is a thinking computer sitting on top of, but not well connected to, a feeling computer. Although this emotional brain is highly sophisticated in perceiving and generating positive and negative feelings, it probably has the IQ of a toddler, able to understand only one- or two-word sentences. The brain systems that control conscious, intentional muscle movement (as opposed to reflexive actions, such as jumping away from a hot stove) are in the thinking brain and are well interconnected with thinking systems. As a result, your thoughts can control your actions. But the thinking brain doesn't know much more about what's happening in the feeling brain than it knows about what's happening in the kidneys. The thinking brain can't just decide to start, stop, or change our feelings. Feeling systems function without much input from our thinking brains, more like stomachs do.

As such, your thinking brain could remind you a thousand times before a presentation that you were exceptionally well-prepared and, therefore, shouldn't feel anxious. Unfortunately, your feeling brain isn't well connected to your thinking brain, so it wouldn't get the message. And even if it did, because your feeling brain doesn't have access to your intelligent thinking brain, your emotional system doesn't have the intelligence to understand what you think or say or want it to do.

In sum, traditional self-help methods aren't able to get your feeling brain to release core confidence. You could think positively and repeat affirmations endlessly, and your emotional system wouldn't understand—so it wouldn't stop generating anxiety. Trying to think or talk your emotional brain into feeling more confident is like trying to talk yourself out of feeling hungry. Your emotional brain isn't able to respond well to reasoning.

The feeling brain's limited structural connection to the thinking brain also explains why negative facts known to the thinking brain, such as "I'm a 25-year-old college dropout living in a van," don't necessarily stop that individual's feeling brain from generating a strong sense of confidence that his invaluable talents entitle him to a great job with good pay.

This feeling brain disconnection helps me understand my struggles with public speaking. From early high school I never felt confident giving a speech or lecture. My entire body felt tense and I often sweated through the armpits of my suit. My father was a confident, excellent public speaker and told me that speaking well contributed greatly to career success. He was also unusually kind, supportive, and helpful, so he often reminded me that his college speech teacher had taught him that the secret to feeling confident while speaking was to just remind yourself to open the mouth, breathe deeply, and have something to say. For ten years I wondered why this secret didn't help me at all. To support myself in graduate school and to build my confidence and skill as a speaker, I chose to teach general psychology. I thought that, at minimum, I would eventually just get so used to speaking that my anxiety would gradually go away.

By my early 40s, I had presented over 2,000 classes, speeches, and seminars—and my armpits were still soaked every time. My batting average for the traditional approach to building confidence was 0 for 2,000.

As for building my skills, without the confidence to relax and exude genuine enthusiasm and spontaneity, my performance was never better than B+. A standing ovation was a laughable notion.

Around midnight one night, as I was writing approximately my 2001st talk, I sat back and asked myself, "Why do you continue to accept these speaking opportunities? You're preparing 50 hours for a one-hour seminar that will soak you in sweat and will rate a B+ at best."

By this time, I had spent 12 years—more than a thousand sessions—in personal psychotherapy, primarily to become the world's best psychologist by learning everything I could about my mind and unconscious feelings. Although I didn't expect to ever come close to that goal, that didn't stop my inner drive to get to the top of the pecking order. In the process, I also was hoping to build my confidence.

That evening, all my years of training, examining clients' feelings, and looking very closely at my own feelings brought an epiphany. I couldn't think of a reason why I kept grinding away at this speaking thing in the face of repeated disappointment, and my attention turned back to writing. A few moments later I noticed a curious little feeling of tension in my chest. After another few moments, I recognized that tiny feeling was excitement. I was writing at midnight because some part of my emotional system was generating excitement and a feeling that if I just persisted, I would give a great lecture.

At which point I laughed aloud and said, "Mother of God and holy Saint Joseph, Bernie. You're 0 for 2,000. How could you possibly expect success? You're a moron."

And that moron, I realized, was the answer. The rational, thinking part of my brain didn't even know about that core confidence. My emotional brain that understands only one- or two-word sentences like "stop," "go," and "eat" generated my confidence. It didn't understand my thoughts or the facts or the reality of failure. It didn't understand 2,000 failures. It wouldn't understand 50,000 failures. It evolved to provide the chutzpah that let my ancestors bring all their strengths and talent to bear in every challenge. It helped them survive. Its biological mandate was to generate one simple pure feeling that I would give a great speech, and nothing else.

I realized that this feeling brain system was generating confidence right at that moment, and that it would still be in my brain when I was speaking. All I needed to do was figure out how to tap into it when I needed it.

Two Distinct Types of Confidence

Combining information from neuropsychology and evolutionary psychology, I began to think about confidence in a new way. If our thinking brains evolved only about 100,000 years ago, it's likely that our feeling brains generated the necessary confidence that evolved over the millions of years prior to that. I believe that there are two distinct forms or types of confidence: traditional confidence and core confidence.

Traditional confidence (or lack of it) results from our experiences and our environmental influences, especially the evaluations we receive from others and the assessments we make of ourselves. In other words, it develops based on how others think of us and treat us and how we think of ourselves. The love, acceptance, and success we have enjoyed and the neglect, rejection, criticism, mistreatment, failure, and mistakes that we have suffered influence this type of confidence. In traditional theories, evaluations of our actions and the experiences that we have are the major influences on confidence. I believe that these thoughts, evaluations, and environmental events stimulate a system in our feeling brains different from our core confidence system and that this traditional system can generate only a mild feeling of confidence.

The second type of confidence—core confidence—is a more central and more powerful inborn emotional experience of self-worth, strength, and importance. It is likely that this primitive system was in place before language and thought. Instead of "I think I can, I think I can," this feeling based confidence system generates a likely nonverbal emotional and possibly visual fantasy of worth and success. Core confidence isn't learned or developed, and it doesn't depend on love, acceptance, or success any more than hunger and thirst do. This innate sense of worth and ability is like hunger, so deeply and permanently part of our nature that it is undamaged by even lifelong neglect, failure, or criticism.

We're born with this primitive, emotional brain system that automatically generates the same confidence which made our ancestors feel they could face a giant beast with a sharpened stick. This confidence should rise inside us as effortlessly as do hunger or sexual desire. Again, I hypothesize that this brain system is separate from the traditional confidence system that is stimulated by thinking and environmental experiences.

Both types of confidence are valuable. Thinking-based confidence is like a water fountain. You can decide to turn it on to refresh yourself, and you can probably fix it if it hasn't been constructed well. Core confidence is a geyser. It never needs fixing. You might partially or totally suppress it by covering it with thick layers of concrete, but it would still be rumbling underneath.

To me, inborn confidence explains how, after winning his first bout, 12-year-old Cassius Clay (later Muhammad Ali) could throw his arms in the air and proclaim, "I will be the greatest of all time." It explains why 21-year-old unknown Pablo Picasso entitled his first art showing in Paris, "I, Picasso!"

Your powerful inborn confidence is untouched by facts or reality. Logic and reason don't exist for this primitive instinct, nor do doubt and failure. Thinking-based efforts to build confidence are like endlessly throwing wood on a campfire to hold back the darkness. Uncovering your deepest belief in yourself is the sun rising inside you. Core confidence excites and empowers you with the feeling that you're taller, stronger, and smarter; that you can do anything. Core confidence generates only one expectation—triumph.

MIT behavioral economist Dan Ariely, author of *Predictably Irrational,* writes that we all sense that our intuitive understanding of ourselves and the world is right, and this certainty causes us to subconsciously resist information that contradicts our understanding. If you've experienced long-term insecurity, my assertion that you unconsciously possess bulletproof core confidence likely contradicts your intuitive understanding.

I don't ask that you blindly believe me. I invite you to explore whether something that seems so different from your experience could be true. Could you feel insecure and yet unconsciously possess strong confidence? Could you feel it and still be a nice person? I believe the answer is yes.

In the first years of my practice, I complained to my colleagues that I thought too many of my clients were not improving or improving too slowly even though I was certain my strategies and interventions were good. Reviewing my approach, my colleagues concurred that it was sound and my success rate was good. They said that, unfortunately, many clients were unable or unwilling to do what was necessary to progress. This was comfortably consistent with my intuitive understanding. Thoughts that I might be unconsciously undermining my clients' progress were uncomfortable and contradicted my experience. Remaining open to contradictory possibilities allowed me to discover that my strong desire for my clients to improve was causing me to unconsciously push them to improve. They unconsciously resisted my pressure in a number of ways, such as procrastinating or forgetting their appointments. Remaining open to contradictory information has helped me enormously, and I believe it will also help you to gain much from this book.

Our Instinctive Confidence Crusher

If core confidence is so automatic, why do so few of us consciously experience it? Wondering about the feelings that helped our ancestors survive led me to suspect that ancestors with feeling brain systems that controlled or suppressed intense confidence would have a survival advantage. Although confidence to the point of fearlessness helped our ancestors survive in many situations, in other circumstances it might have made them believe they could leap a 30-foot crevasse, kill a mammoth barehanded, or fight a dozen invaders alone, thus ensuring extinction.

Also, uncontrolled swaggering and conceit would have alienated our ancestors' friends and allies, thereby weakening their family and tribal units. Humans, like most other species, compete to be at the top of the pecking order—to be the alpha male or female. But if everyone constantly felt that he or she were superior and should lead, constant combat and chaos would result. I believe that tribes survived more effectively when only a few released the enormous sense of worth and importance that propelled them to fight for leadership. Thus tribes in which leadership-inspiring confidence was spread along a continuum from high to low would have a survival advantage. Societies would work best with the king or queen at the high confidence/leadership end of the confidence continuum, followed by some individuals exuding enough confidence to achieve middle levels of leadership and power. Then the docile rest would exist at the low confidence end, at the cooperative worker bee level, so to speak.

My observations of my clients and of people in general over thirty years of practice indicate that the amount of core confidence we consciously feel varies along a bell-shaped continuum. At one end of the continuum, the lucky few freely exude core confidence. At the other end, unlucky individuals suppress all or most of their confidence. These latter would have no awareness of their underlying confidence or their suppressive system.

For years I've watched hundreds of clients unconsciously suppress one intense feeling, such as anger, by unconsciously generating another strong feeling, such as sadness, anxiety, or depression. They would feel sad or anxious in situations that would naturally stimulate anger. Once they became more comfortable with their suppressed anger, they stopped generating sadness and were able to consciously feel their anger and channel it productively.

I began to suspect that a similar suppressive emotional system caused individuals to remain at the low confidence/worker bee level. I watched countless clients feel uneasy after receiving a compliment, such as "That's an important insight." Instead of enjoying it, they undermined it by generating a self-critical feeling. They'd say something negative, such as "It doesn't make up for being an idiot."

I often restated the compliment and asked if they experienced even a mildly good feeling about themselves. Rarely could they do so. One client responded to my question about his college grade point average by saying, "Three-point-nine, but I'm not that smart. I just work hard."

Several clients declined higher-paying job opportunities because they were too anxious about making the required speeches or presentations. They thought that they were afraid of criticism or failure, but this made no sense. They weren't going to fail, because they were highly intelligent and exceptionally articulate. They would have been experts speaking to audiences that were less informed and expecting to be educated. Nobody would have known if my clients *had* made a mistake. Their feeling so insecure didn't add up.

When I stepped back and looked at the situations in which my clients felt insecure, I saw a pattern. They felt these negative emotions in situations in which they knew the most. They had everyone's attention. They were in control, taking charge. They were top dog. Theoretically, these situations should have stimulated strong feelings of instinctive worth and importance: "I'm smart, and you will want to listen to the valuable things I have to say." Why was a confidence-stimulating situation producing the opposite of confidence? It seemed likely that something was going on in their feeling brains. Before they could feel confidence at a conscious level, a primitive control system in their feeling brains generated anxiety and self-doubt in order to suppress their inborn confidence.

As in most people, my clients' suppressive brain systems were stuck at the worker-bee setting, restricting their belief in their own strength and importance. A number of these clients used my Confidence Release Technique to relax or desensitize their suppressive systems. The empowering biological belief in themselves eventually surged through them, and they were finally able to live their lives without the paralysis of insecurity. One client (who felt so insecure that introducing himself to a small group of his co-workers gave him panic attacks) uncovered so much primal confidence that a year later he was eager to give a presentation to five hundred co-workers and superiors.

When I first thought about which brain activities might generate confidence or its suppression, I visualized separate areas of the brain creating these feelings. It was the easiest way to picture the situation. Because brain functioning is so complex and controversial, what we *don't* know about it exceeds all that we do know. We don't yet know, for example, why certain antidepressants work for some patients and not for others.

It's unclear whether core confidence and corresponding suppressive feelings are generated by localized brain centers or through widely dispersed brain activity. For our purposes, it doesn't matter. To make things easy, I'll refer to the brain activities that generate confidence or suppression as "systems," denoting either a system of cellular response patterns that are widely dispersed in the brain or fully contained in a defined brain center. Accordingly, Figure 1 shows a symbolic dark suppressive system with layers of negative feelings covering and paralyzing our survival instincts, including core confidence.

Think of the primitive control system in our ancestors' emotional brain as similar to the thermostat that controls the air conditioning in your house. If your thermostat is set to turn on the air conditioning at sixty degrees, then it turns on the air conditioning when the temperature reaches sixty degrees, no matter how badly you want the house to be warm. Most of us are born with suppressive systems that are set to allow only a low intensity of primal confidence because that had survival value for our ancestors.

The moment our confidence heats up past this level, our suppressive system makes a misguided effort to protect us from what it registers as dangerous confidence. It instantly floods the feeling brain with feelings that we're not smart, witty, or attractive enough. We end up tense, worried, or sweating.

At this point in our evolution, we have thinking brains capable of controlling our actions, and we no longer need this archaic suppressive control system to crush our confidence. Remember that the movement centers in your brain are close to and well connected to your thinking brain. So no matter what you feel, your intelligent thinking brain can decide to act with common sense. Unfortunately, the suppressive system still needlessly paralyzes our confidence with insecurity and self-doubt or chokes it off with anxiety and self-criticism.

Now I'll show you a symbolic way to grasp how debilitating it is to suppress your core confidence. Imagine that your left arm and hand represent your core confidence and your right arm and hand represent your kindness, empathy, and humility. To symbolically represent your suppressive system's influence, imagine that in order to control your core confidence, your suppressive system has you unconsciously bending down and stepping on your left hand. In addition, imagine that as your suppressive system is making you live your life while standing on your left hand, it also won't let you have any awareness of your core confidence. Wave your right arm and say out loud, "I'm a good person. I don't like cocky people. I only feel kind and humble. I have this nice arm on the right side of my body." What a debilitating way to live!

Now stand up and raise both arms powerfully. Can you still decide to act nicely and friendly, not cocky? If you recognized and accepted all of your survival instincts, would you feel stronger and more able to live powerfully and successfully?

Few of us escape suppression. Even talented people who appear completely confident are often unsure of themselves, living with the vague feeling that they're missing some key strength. Many successful people secretly feel like imposters and believe they are constantly in danger of being found out. F. Scott Fitzgerald, one of the most successful novelists of his time, wrote that at his core he lacked the essentials and had "no real courage, perseverance, or self-respect." It's likely that you don't feel inadequate or have low self-esteem because you have failed or been criticized. I believe that your suppressive system creates at least eighty percent of the insecurity and self-doubt you feel. Less than twenty percent comes from the failure and criticism you have endured over the course of your life.

Most of us can't feel our core confidence system surging to power us through presentations, job interviews, or other high-pressure situations. Our emotional governors are stuck worrying we'll create problems if we brag too much in the cave, unaware that we now possess rational thought to choose safe, sensible actions to express our confidence. Suppression hasn't caught up to our evolution.

If you don't feel confident, it's likely that hidden deep in your brain an archaic suppressive system prevents you from accessing your primitive belief in yourself. That primitive belief is a regal confidence, equal to that of Winston Churchill or Barack Obama.

Wouldn't you like to uncover and relish your "Yes, I can" feeling?

Core Confidence Will Not Make You Conceited

Dave was a very bright and friendly 35-year-old who said, "It just doesn't feel right that I should encourage biological confident beliefs. If I felt terrific about myself, wouldn't I start acting self-important?"

A year later, after he had relaxed his suppressive system into releasing his core confidence and felt much less anxious and depressed, he told me, "At first, core confidence felt terribly not right, but I can see that it is right and that core confidence makes me stronger and less confused and wimpy. I'm more assertive at work and in my marriage, and my relationships in both are much better. I easily control my actions and choose not to offend anyone. I still want to be kind and considerate toward others and want them to like and respect me, but I know when and how to assert myself, too."

If you're worried that core confidence might make you conceited, rest assured that these feelings are easy to control. Even if you feel tremendous confidence, it will not lessen your desire to be liked and respected.

You also can choose how you act no matter what you feel inside. You can feel core confidence and still act appropriately (if you want hard evidence now, skip to Chapter 4). Remember, you have a big thinking brain, and that thinking brain will know that the benefits of acting sensibly and diplomatically far outweigh the short-term pleasure of acting arrogantly. Haven't you felt strong sexual feelings while standing near a gorgeous person? And yet, you were easily able to control your desire to grab him or her, right?

Even as a teenager, Muhammad Ali controlled his strong ego and was civil to everyone, including his teachers.

On *60 Minutes*, refreshingly unpretentious actor Michael Caine said that all actors are enormously egotistical. "I simply hide it very, very, well," he said.

Mark Twain said, "Good breeding consists of concealing how much we think of ourselves and how little we think of the other fellow."

People who release core confidence don't need to convince themselves and others that they're important. They know that acting conceited or haughty offends others and damages relationships. Because confident people feel good about themselves, they are happier and more fulfilled. Happy people are kinder and more considerate than unhappy people.

Conceited People Have Faulty Brain Systems

If raw confidence can't make you *act* conceited, what drives arrogant people? I believe the vast majority of those who act arrogantly have brains that function differently. They don't recognize how much conceit they're exuding, and they don't recognize that they're offending others.

Conceited people's brains don't seem to generate the normal level of compassion for other people, so they don't really care whether or not they're offensive. In other words, they suffer from a lack of empathy. Jean M. Twenge, Ph.D., and W. Keith Campbell, Ph.D., reviewed recent research in their fascinating book on narcissism (a psychological term for conceit). This research demonstrates that at both a conscious and unconscious level, self-centered or narcissistic people feel exceptionally good about themselves. They are not, as commonly thought, compensating for insecurity. Unfortunately, they consciously and unconsciously don't value kindness, generosity, or other compassionate traits. They also have a neutral to negative attitude toward closeness and emotional intimacy with others.

If you're concerned about acting conceited, it's likely that your brain does generate insight and concern for others and also a desire for closeness and good relationships with them. Any one of these feelings is enough to make you avoid acting arrogantly even when feeling the strongest core confidence.

Surprisingly, your ability to uncover and release instinctive confidence depends primarily on whether or not you feel that you can control it. You must recognize and then teach your suppressive system that you can feel enormous confidence and still decide to act friendly and appropriate.

To be free of self-doubt, insecurity, and self-criticism, you never have to act arrogantly. You never even have to mention that you feel confident. You only have to feel core confidence inside your body. To enjoy the empowering strength and vitality of your deepest belief in yourself, you need only the openness, honesty, and integrity to look inside yourself and respect your core confidence.

Core Confidence Will Not Make You Delusional

Are you afraid that if you feel really good about yourself you'll develop a distorted sense of your true abilities? Don't worry. Your thinking brain is still vigilantly assessing what you should and shouldn't do. You know you could lose, fail, or get rejected. But that knowledge in your thinking brain doesn't stop the flow of core confidence in your feeling brain from pumping you up. You can feel great about yourself and still act sensibly.

Unleashing my inborn confidence didn't make me smarter than Einstein or stronger than Superman. It won't guarantee that you'll win or succeed either. But it will let you harness all your strength and talent to pursue your goals, per form as well as you can, and have a rip-roaring good time doing it. Unleashing your confidence will give you your best chance in life.

When you feel really good about yourself, your confidence will be positively reflected in your body language: you'll smile more, you'll stand taller, and you'll project infectious energy and enthusiasm. Your body will be saying that you feel really good about yourself, that you like and respect other people, and that you want to have a fine relationship with them.

These qualities are exciting and attractive to others. If your body language sends out messages that you enjoy life, respect your friends, and feel good about yourself, you'll draw lots of people and select the best ones as friends.

New Techniques to Release Core Confidence

Because of the limited connection between our feeling and thinking brains, I wanted to develop methods for helping clients to feel their core confidence that didn't rely on logic or facts. Instead, I determined to develop techniques using feelings and visualizations so simple that the primitive suppressive system could grasp them and then relax and release core confidence.

I started with the person I knew best: myself. Two decades ago, I began designing visualizations—I call them "fancy daydreams"—to relax my suppressive system. These visualizations filled my emotional system with a strong feeling of my commitment to my morals and ethics and my desire to keep my life on track by acting sensibly. They created a pervasive emotional atmosphere that made my suppressive system relax and release my deepest belief in myself. It worked.

Getting out from under the boot heel of self-doubt is indescribably relieving. It's also the foundation upon which my other personal and professional successes and experiences now stand.

I have been testing and improving this visualization program over the last 20 years in about 25,000 client sessions. It's presented in Chapter 7. You, too, can use it to unleash your core confidence.

When you're facing a presentation, a job interview, or a personal confrontation, you can't know in advance whether or not you will triumph. You need a belief in yourself that feels bulletproof even if there are no facts to justify it. Core confidence will make you calm, poised, and will help you bring all your strength and talent to bear in meeting your goal.

A lucky few believe in themselves so deeply that their flaws and failures are forgotten as they are swept toward success by the power of their core confidence. Babe Didrickson Zaharias, great female golfer of the 1940s, often remarked to other competitors before a match, "Well, girls, who's going to come in second?"

Wouldn't it be great to feel the confidence that made Beethoven profess, "There is only one Beethoven," and Babe Ruth stand at the plate, pointing his bat where he intended to slam his next home run? No matter how much confidence you release, you probably won't play as well as Ruth or compose as well as Beethoven. But if you release your instinctive sense of your own strength and talent and stop tying your emotional system in a knot with suppressive feelings, you can really rock and roll. In an interview on the *Tonight Show*, Robin Williams said, "If I can get out of my own way, I can be really funny."

When I was young, I dearly wanted to leave my anxiety behind and step up to the plate eager to swing big and relish the experience, win or lose. For the next three decades I often felt tense at dances, parties, social events, job interviews, lectures, confrontations, negotiations, client sessions, and all other challenges big and small. I tried hard to believe in myself enough to enjoy these experiences.

I've learned that you don't have to struggle for confidence. All you have to do is not be afraid to see and accept all that you actually feel deep inside: that you're not only a nice, humble, friendly person, you're also brimming with a bulletproof sense of your own worth, strength, and talent. When you see and accept core confidence, everything else seems to fall into place.

Once released, core confidence makes you see yourself in an entirely new way. You escape worry, self-doubt, nervousness, and feelings of inadequacy. Even under heavy pressure, instead of having a dry mouth, cold hands, wet armpits, pounding heart, queasy stomach, or that irritating lump in your throat, you can feel genuinely comfortable in your own skin.

If you don't release your natural confidence, your struggle to escape self-doubt and anxiety will likely go on for the rest of your life. You may never believe in yourself enough to project the poise that makes others have faith in you. Your list of unfulfilled dreams and failed expectations may go on and on: Lost opportunities, stunted performances, failure to stand up for yourself, reluctance to ask for a raise, and not even trying to reach for your dream job, dream date, or dream home.

The only way to really understand what you are missing is to uncover your deepest belief in yourself. To do that, we'll take a look at the real you.

References

Ariely, D. (2008). *Predictably irrational*. New York: Harper Collins.

Barkley, R. (2011). *Executive functioning: Impairments and treatment*. Online presentation http://www.caddac.ca/cms/video/teens_adults_player.html.

Churchill Centre and Museum at the Cabinet War Rooms, London. (n.d.). Biography section. Retrieved from website http://www.winston churchill. org

De Waal, F. (2005). Our inner ape. New York: Riverhead Books.

Gilbert, M. (1994). *In search of Churchill: a historian's journey*. London: Harper Collins. Pg. 215.

Greenwald, A. (1992). New look 3: Unconscious cognition reclaimed. *American Psychologist, 47,* 766-79.

Gregory, S. W., and Webster, S. (1996). "A nonverbal signal in voices of interview partners effectively predicts communication accommodation and social status perceptions." *Journal of Personality and Social Psychology, 70,* 1231-1240.

Gregory, S. W., and Gallagher, T. J. (2002). "Spectral analysis of candidates' nonverbal vocal communication: predicting US presidential election outcomes." *Social Psychology Quarterly, 65,* 298-308.

Loftus, E., & Klinger, M. (1992). Is the unconscious smart or dumb? *American Psychologist, 47,* 761-65.

Manchester, W. (1983). *The last lion: William Spencer Churchill*. Boston: Little, Brown & Co.

Remnick, D. (1998). *King of the world*. New York: Random House.

Sharot, T. (2011). *The optimism bias*. New York: Pantheon Books. Pg. xv.

Sperling, D. (1989). *Michael Jordan: Come fly with me.* New York: NBA Entertainment.

Trivers, R. (2000). The elements of a scientific theory of self-deception. *Annals NY Acad. Sciences* 907:114-31.

Trivers, R. (2010). Deceit and self-deception. In P. Kappeler & J. Silk (Eds.), *Mind the Gap.* Berlin: Springer-Verlag.

Twenge, J., & Campbell, W. (2009). *The narcissism epidemic.* New York: Free Press.

Whitaker, M. 1998. *Michael Jordan unauthorized: A collection of quotes in four quarters.* Chicago: Bonus Books.

Williamson, M. (1992). *A return to love.* New York: Harper Collins.

Wood, J., Perunovic, W., & Lee, J. (2009). Positive self statements: Power for some, peril for others. *Psychological Science, 20,* 860-66.

Wrangham, R. (1991). Is military incompetence adaptive? *Evolution and Human Behavior* (20.1) 3-17.

CHAPTER 2

The Neuroanatomy of Self-Confidence

"You have to think you're the greatest thing since sliced bread, but you have to know that you're not."

— Bette Midler

Will you look back on your life when you're 80 years old and regret that you never felt comfortable in your own skin, never met a group of strangers without cold hands or a dry mouth, never stopped needing approval from a boss, spouse, parent, or partner?

This doesn't have to be you. Instead you can relish the bulletproof belief in yourself that may have inspired Goethe to write, "Whatever you can do, or dream you can, begin it. Boldness has genius, power, and magic in it."

As discussed in Chapter One, there are centers deep in the *feeling* brain, completely beneath the awareness of the conscious, *thinking* mind, that generate core confidence automatically. Situations such as deadlines, sales presentations, athletic events, and social settings automatically stimulate the feeling system to generate a core confidence and passion similar to what Teddy Roosevelt called "the wolf rising in the heart."

The brain suppresses most of this hot-blooded core confidence in order to control it. But, it simmers deep inside us, bequeathed by countless generations of gutsy men and women. It has survived through thousands of years because it made us believe in ourselves blindly, feel invincible, and charge toward victory with no thought of defeat. And it's perfectly, perfectly, perfectly safe to feel even your deepest belief in yourself.

A Closer Look at Your Confidence Suppressing System

One of my clients, Nia, a young woman with big brown eyes, short hair, and a friendly smile, had trained three hours a day for three years to compete in national fitness competitions. She did well in the minor events but had never performed well in the all-important floor routine. She felt stiff, self-conscious, and uneasy in front of people, and always hurried to finish and get off stage.

She had no idea why she couldn't overcome these insecurities. She knew that she was strong and attractive, and she also knew that she was talented and extremely well-prepared. She hired a top choreographer to help her design a routine that should have kept the audience on the edge of their seats. But she failed where success counted most. She was afraid that she just didn't "have what it takes."

I asked her to imagine performing in slow motion so that she could study her feelings closely. At first she was conscious only of feeling stiff and uneasy, but finally she noticed some hidden feelings:

"*I'm-a-nobody-just-showing-off-trying-to-make-people-think-I'm-cool.*" Ouch!

Traditional theory proposes that these feelings developed as she incorporated early criticism, rejection, and failure into a basic sense of herself as flawed and inadequate. In fact, she had plenty of these painful experiences as a child. The traditional therapy is to confront and remove these negative beliefs and build new, more accurate beliefs about her strength and value.

The traditional treatment engages the client's thinking mind to confront and remove these negative beliefs and build new, more accurate beliefs about the client's strength and value. This cognitive approach can produce changes in a separate, less powerful, thinking-based confidence system. However, I have never seen this approach deliver core confidence, the bulletproof belief in yourself that most of us want.

Nia is so much more than an insecure woman struggling to overcome her weaknesses. She was born a powerful creature with fiery passions and unfathomable strengths, including an indomitable belief in herself. She already possessed instinctive confidence, but it was camouflaged by insecurity.

Intense competitions stimulated Nia's core confidence system to arouse the same instinctive sense of importance and desire to be the center of attention that a 4-year-old feels while performing for her parents: "Look at me! I'm terrific!" Before Nia could feel this confidence consciously, however, it alarmed her suppressive system, triggering it to fill her with anxiety and self-doubt instead.

As I watched this disciplined woman endure repeated failures, I thought that no one who truly believed at her core that she "didn't have what it takes" would work so hard and invest so much time and money. No, somewhere underneath all her debilitating insecurities, a powerful part of her was shouting, "I can do this. Let me do my stuff! I'll make 'em stand up and cheer!"

To uncover this primitive self-worth, I began a series of visual exercises (presented in Chapter Seven) to persuade Nia's suppressive system to stop injecting self-criticism. I guided her through visualizations that showed her suppressive system vivid images of herself feeling cool and confident, yet still strongly preferring to act normally, not haughty or conceited. We recorded these visualizations, and she listened to them several times a week.

After three weeks of exposing her suppressive system to these reassuring visual images, Nia was looking at herself in the mirrored gym wall, and for the first time in her life, she felt electrified: I look terrific. I rock! Goosebumps stood out all over her body. Then, three or four seconds later, she felt a crushing feeling, "Yeah, but your routine still sucks!" She was so depressed that she couldn't even finish her workout.

She wondered why the negative feelings had returned. The visualizations had relaxed her suppressive system enough that, for a few seconds, it allowed raw core confidence to surge. But this feeling quickly alarmed her suppressive system into again paralyzing her with criticism. When clients begin Confidence Release Technique, they feel brief moments of confidence, but as these feelings of confidence get more intense, they are quickly suppressed again until the suppressive system relaxes even more with additional visualizations.

I recorded another visualization to help Nia imagine performing while safely enjoying electrifying, *"I-look-terrific, I-can-do-anything"* feelings surging through her body. She repeatedly exposed her suppressive system to them several times each week. Gradually, her confidence surfaced more often and stayed longer. A few months later, she felt bulletproof throughout her performance and placed first in all three of her events.

This was the first of numerous successes for Nia. She quickly became very confident in the regional meets. However, when facing the strongest competitors in the biggest national contests, she again felt nervous and self-critical. These important contests stimulated much more intense core confidence. Once her suppressive system warmed up to this deeper, more intense confidence, she became so successful that she turned professional. Corporations sponsored her to compete in national professional fitness contests, and now she coaches and consults with athletes.

We usually think of our brains as response machines. They do their work by acting and creating. We never think of them as systems working to inhibit the responses of other primitive in-house systems. But much of our brain function is inhibitory. I remember a neuroimaging study demonstrating that our brains are actually working harder when we sit still, in other words, working hard to inhibit our natural impulses to move and act.

Recent neuroimaging research shows that the anterior or forward part of the cingulate gyrus—a brain structure running along the top and front of the brains limbic (emotional) system—inhibits or suppresses emotional responses. Russell A. Barkley, Ph.D., a clinical professor of psychiatry at the Medical University of South Carolina, is an internationally recognized authority on ADHD in children and adults. Dr. Barkley recently summarized a review of neuroimaging research over the last ten years by George Bush, M.D., MMSc, a neuro-imager and associate professor of psychiatry at Harvard Medical School and the director of the Massachusetts General Hospital Cingulate Cortex Research Laboratory. In addition to showing that the anterior cingulate inhibits emotional responses, this research also showed that individuals with ADHD have a smaller anterior cingulate and that their brains don't inhibit emotional responses nearly as well. I believe that individuals with great confidence were born with suppressive systems that don't inhibit high levels of instinctive confidence. Some of us have highly sensitive suppressive systems that are set so low that even mild levels of confidence will trigger them to flood us with insecurities. As a result, we feel no confidence at all. If your suppressive system is moderately sensitive, you'll feel some shaky confidence before your suppressive system turns on negative feelings. Nia's suppressive system was moderately sensitive. She used the Confidence Release Technique visualizations to become comfortable with her own more intense feelings of confidence.

Clients need repeated reassurance before they are able to feel safe releasing their core confidence. They cling to the feeling that suppression is a good thing that keeps their "bad arrogance" under control. I believe that the evolution of the thinking brain made our suppressive system obsolete. No matter how much confidence you release, your thinking brain will still know you can't stop a speeding locomotive, and it will prevent you from wagering your life savings that you will win the next sales, baking, or athletic contest. Though you will understand that you could lose, you'll still feel that you will win, and this belief in yourself will energize and empower you to perform your best.

Core Confidence Is Easily Controlled

You have two methods of controlling your core confidence: your suppressive system, an unconscious, reflexive, and irrational system that chokes off your confidence, and your intelligent conscious mind that stops only conceited actions while allowing your primitive belief in yourself to empower you.

Let's say your core confidence system generates the feeling that your solution to a group problem is the best, and everyone should follow it. To control this raw confidence, your suppressive system makes you feel so insecure that, even if you can muster the courage to mention your solution, your body language conveys nervousness or unease. This suppression isn't necessary—no matter how intensely confident you feel, your thinking mind will know that it's better to present your ideas diplomatically and appropriately. Without the suppression, your body language will radiate poise and power.

Even though we no longer need our suppressive system, we are genetically stuck with it. It's so powerful that traditional efforts to build confidence with logic, positive thinking, or other thinking-based techniques are like shoveling sand against the tide. The suppressive system can learn to change, but it responds to visualizations and feelings, not thinking.

Nature vs. Nurture

In the 1970s I thoroughly believed, as the majority of psychologists did, that our personalities were determined primarily by parental training and other environmental influences. In recent years, research increasingly indicates that biology and genetics determine our personalities as much as or more than environmental influences.

For example, the personality development of identical twins separated shortly after birth and raised in dramatically different environments has been studied extensively. In one case, one twin was raised in a loving, accepting, and nurturing family and the other in a colder and more critical family. Surprisingly, the twins developed similar personalities, including very specific traits, such as smoking, insomnia, alcoholism, thumb-sucking, bed-wetting, nail-biting, hypochondria, political orientation, depth of religious experience, and fear of the dark.

Core confidence theory contends that the biological structure of your suppressive system primarily determines how confident you feel. Most of us are born with overly sensitive suppressive systems that paralyze much of our belief in ourselves. Supremely confident people are born with suppressive systems that don't constrict raw confidence.

Young children often exude an illogical, core confidence before their suppressive systems develop anatomically. A 4-year-old's core confidence system can generate an intense belief: *"I-can-drive-the-car. Let-me-drive!"* You explain she can't reach the pedals, but she still absolutely believes she can drive. My Confidence Release Technique relaxes or desensitizes your suppressive system until it releases your core confidence.

Core confidence systems can't effectively think or evaluate facts, such as how inexperienced you are or how much bigger, smarter, or better-looking your competition is. So even if your logical mind knows the odds are against you, you will still feel bulletproof.

Even if your company has lost $300,000, you're almost out of money, and personal bankruptcy is looming at your doorstep, core confidence can help you survive, as it did one of my clients. Jim felt gloomy and anxious every day. I told him the best, and possibly the only chance for him to perform well enough to save his company required setting the facts aside and focusing only on letting his core confidence empower him.

Jim and I both knew, rationally, this feeling might not save his company. However, his gloom and anxiety lifted when his suppressive system stopped paralyzing his biological sense that he was a creative genius who could not fail. His energy returned, and ingenious solutions popped into his mind. He didn't become delusional and start thinking he was superhuman. He only felt like a genius. But the feeling allowed him to perform at his best and save his company.

To understand the delicious physical sensation of confidence that your suppressive system has always repressed, imagine that you were born with a small brain system that constantly pumped a numbing anesthetic, such as Novocain or Xylocain, into your tongue, with the result that you had never experienced the full delight of Ben and Jerry's ice cream. Now, imagine that you were able to persuade your brain system to stop infusing the anesthetic, and you tasted Chocolate Chunk for the very first time. "Wow!" doesn't even begin to describe it, right? Calming your suppressive system enough to release your confidence is even more delightful and much more deeply gratifying.

This free-flowing, inborn confidence is so much more powerful than thinking we are lovable, valuable, or good enough. Core confidence unsuppressed by self-doubt is truly the sun rising within you.

We mistakenly believe the thinking brain can produce this core confidence by consciously developing a belief system of positive thoughts about ourselves, which we call "self-confidence." Thinking-based confidence is the lightning bug; feeling-based core confidence is the lightning bolt.

Confidence Release Technique will desensitize your suppressive system, allowing it to relax and let your confidence centers pump you full of an *"I-am-magic"* feeling. This isn't a simple or easy process. Some will be able to master it in a few weeks. For most, it will require months.

Your Brain Rebels Against Pressure

One of the most fascinating things I have learned in my thirty years as a psychologist is that human beings have a deep resistance to pressure, even the slightest implied pressure. An unusually intelligent student came to see me because he was studying hard and could not understand why he had flunked out of two colleges. It became clear that he unconsciously both hated his father's pressure to get high grades and relished rebelling against him.

I have seen numerous frustrated salespeople angry at themselves because they won't make calls or finish paperwork. When I call their attention to the momentary rebellious grin that slips out as they describe themselves "not doing anything," they have no awareness of feeling rebellious. Usually, it takes only a session or two before they can feel their resistance and another session before they express rebellious feelings: "Nobody pushes me. I'm not doing anything." Once they stop pushing themselves, they start selling fast.

Because you don't even know you're resisting, this discussion may seem irrelevant. However, resistance (termed "psychological reactance" by experimental psychologists) is a universal human trait. I believe it's a minor problem for a few people and the difference between failure and success for well over half the population. It's best to get it on the table at the start.

During the first twelve or so years of working with clients, I watched our efforts to uncover confidence often lead to unexplainable and sometimes permanent inertia. I realized that my strong desire for them to gain confidence ignited an almost imperceptible resistance to my suggestions and, oddly, theirs. They dug in their heels without realizing it.

Even though I've stopped pushing clients, their resistance systems often interpret my enthusiasm for them to uncover their confidence as pushing. As a result, they resist progress even though their thinking brains want it. I cringe at the thought of causing any more rebellious failure. So please know that even if you like the concepts in this book, your resistance can still sense my enthusiasm as pressure and secretly dig in its heels to make you feel frustrated, pessimistic, or some other debilitating emotion.

It's the same in your relationship with yourself. A very large percentage of the people who read this book won't recognize that they are also pushing and even driving themselves to obtain confidence. Eagerness to uncover your instinctive strength is not the same feeling as pushing or driving yourself to do so. These two feelings are likely activated by different brain systems.

Wanting something, even at very intense levels, feels pleasant and anticipatory. Pushing or driving yourself, no matter how subtle or camouflaged, feels uncomfortable. It's impossible to force a human to feel something. If you have enormous power, you may be able to force someone's hand over their head, but you can't make them feel happy about it. If you push yourself to read this book or to uncover your confidence, your resistance may slam and bolt a door deep inside you.

Self-driving is a serious problem holding back many people. I call it the Drill Sergeant. You'll learn how to bypass the Drill Sergeant and access healthy motivation in Chapter Eight.

The Confidence Suppression Test

The following test covers a few of the symptoms that suppressive systems create to deaden core confidence. I included the most frequent statements that my clients and others have made about their experience of living without enough confidence.

I use this test in my practice to quickly identify confidence problems. Any item rated three or greater suggests that your suppressive system may be crippling your confidence in that area. Some individuals' suppressive systems may generate only a few of the symptoms, but these few unremittingly paralyze their confidence.

The more of these symptoms you have, the more core confidence you are probably paralyzing.

Rank how often (on a scale of 0 to 5) you feel the following are true of you:

Never	*Rarely*	*Occasionally*	*Often*	*Very Often*	*Almost Constantly*
0	**1**	**2**	**3**	**4**	**5**

_____I criticize myself.
_____I think about my failures.
_____I feel inadequate.
_____I avoid limelight.
_____I think I'm not living up to my potential.
_____I feel I'm not as confident as I should be.
_____I have a hard time accepting compliments.
_____I am afraid of making mistakes.
_____I feel I'm not as smart as I need to be.
_____I feel I am not reaching the successes I should achieve.
_____I feel insecure.
_____I doubt my decisions.
_____When starting a big challenge, I worry about failing.
_____When I make decisions, I have second thoughts or regrets.
_____I'm not satisfied with my performance.
_____I put myself down.
_____I feel I don't have enough talent.
_____Even when I succeed, I feel it it's not enough.

_____I think people see me as inadequate.

_____I feel I'm not interesting.

_____I feel I don't speak well enough.

_____I feel I should be more organized.

_____I feel I am too fat or too thin.

_____I feel I'm not attractive enough.

_____I feel rejected.

_____I feel I need to improve myself.

_____Others seem to get the best of me.

_____I expect criticism for my performance.

_____I feel I need more backbone.

_____I question my judgment.

_____I feel guilty.

Measuring Your Current Core Confidence

The Baseline Confidence Measure below contains statements designed to stimulate progressively stronger levels of core confidence. After you read each statement, wait a few seconds to let the feeling form inside you and then let it flow out as you say the words out loud.

These statements are not affirmations. They are not designed to persuade you that you should feel confident. We simply want to measure the intensity of raw confidence your suppressive system will allow you to feel before it paralyzes your confidence by making you feel bored, silly, confused, self-conscious, self-critical, or some other distracting or negative feeling. These statements stimulate core confidence processes and invite you to feel them. As you say each statement, note the strength of your confident feeling.

The statements don't have to be true to be helpful, so don't judge them. Just enjoy feeling them whether or not you think they are true. Don't try to sound confident. Trying is mostly pushing yourself, and part of your feeling brain will resist pressure.

Note the number of statements you can say comfortably. Make the first several statements even if you don't consciously notice any confidence.

Stop when your suppressive system makes you feel too bored, silly, confused, distracted, self-critical, or deadens the feeling in your statements. Note how subtly it stops your confidence.

Many people's suppressive system will let them say all the statements but not let them feel much, if any, confidence as they say them.

Mark the last statement that you could say comfortably. Also mark at which statement your feelings started to diminish. As you progress through the book and the accompanying exercises, you may wish to retake the Baseline Confidence Measure frequently because improvements will encourage you.

Baseline Confidence Measure

I am a good person.
I am capable.
I am very capable.
I am exceptionally capable.
I can do anything.
I am terrific and cute, too.
I am the greatest.
I am the greatest of all time.
I am magic.

References

Brehm, J.W. (1966). *A theory of psychological reactance*. New York: Academic Press.

Brehm, S.S. & Brehm, J.W. (1981).*Psychological reactance*. New York: Academic Press.

Wright, L. (1995, August). Double mystery: Recent research into the nature of twins. *The New Yorker, 7,* 45-62.

CHAPTER 3

Uncovering Your
Hidden Dimensions

"There is a certain arrogance of ego that comes with comedy. You have to think you're really good or really different . . . . You don't have to say it to anybody . . . but that's exactly what you need to feel!"

— JAY LENO

Modern research shows that the brain is not one thinking unit. It actually functions more like a collection of independent subsystems. You can see, hear, smell, taste, and touch all at the same time because separate systems perform each of these functions. Each subsystem processes different information and performs its own function without knowing much about the others or the information they process. Because the senses function independently, they enhance our chances for survival. If something happens to one, we can still survive using the others. For example, a stroke can completely destroy speech without injuring vision or touch.

As mentioned in Chapter 1, the brain has two separate parts: an evolved thinking part and a primitive feeling part (see Figure 1). The subsystems forming the thinking brain lie on the outer surface. Though they can function independently, they are well connected to one another.

The older, more primitive feeling part is also composed of subsystems and is similar to the emotional system in animal brains. This feeling part, called the limbic system, lies in the center of the brain. Though it understands feelings well and can generate several feelings simultaneously, it doesn't comprehend verbal thinking or language well. This feeling part controlled much of our ancestor's behavior until the highly intelligent thinking part evolved about 100,000 years ago.

You Feel a Lot More Than You Realize

Sigmund Freud's early claim that 90% of our emotions occur out of our conscious awareness has been supported by research. Most of the brain's activity is carried out beyond the reach of the conscious thinking systems. For example, many of us drive safely while our conscious thoughts are elsewhere. Insights that we commonly call intuition often arise when we process nonverbal information that the conscious thinking brain hasn't noticed, such as body language (nervous fidgeting) or a hint of irritation in someone's voice.

Imagine how overwhelming it would be for the thinking brain to consciously manage all our activities: "OK, now breathe, now chew, now remember not to urinate in your pants, now chew again, now produce sexual arousal, now stop digesting food, and now produce adrenaline." Just as the kidneys function beyond the awareness of the thinking brain, so the emotional brain generates and processes feelings that we can't think about.

With all that's going on in our brains, it's not surprising that we have a hard time knowing why we feel anxious, insecure, or self-critical and why using thinking-based confidence-building techniques, such as affirmations, don't add much confidence. These systems simply don't listen to each other.

Unconscious Mind or Feeling Brain?

In my early college years, I believed Freud's concept of the unconscious mind was unimportant and a little weird. It seems less weird if you think of the brain as a collection of separate systems many of which function outside your awareness. I have seen countless clients hold intense emotions, desires, and images in their emotional brain that are completely out of the awareness of their conscious thinking brain. Extensive research supports this as well. Unconsciously, one feeling brain system can generate core confidence and another can smother it with anxieties, self-doubts, and other negative feelings that we experience as a painful lack of confidence.

The instinctive brain system that automatically enabled our ancestors to remain poised under heavy pressure helped them survive. Wouldn't they be much more likely to win the biggest portion of the kill, the warmest part of the cave, and the strongest and healthiest mate if they felt an unshakable sense of "I am the best, I will win"?

For example, which cavewoman would most likely have become extinct: the woman who gave up her share of the tribe's food to another family or the one who demanded her fair share for herself and her children? These inborn feelings of worth and importance help form pecking orders. In the 1920s, the Norwegian biologist Thorleif Schjelderup-Ebbe coined the term "pecking order" after watching hens peck one another until they had established a social hierarchy. While cooperation is also an important survival instinct, males and females in most species struggle for the alpha position in the group because their bodies fill with the strong desire to be the top dog. Neuropsychologist Karl Pribram demonstrated that an emotional brain center called the amygdala is involved in generating this instinctive drive for dominance. He destroyed the amygdala in the alpha male in a chimpanzee troop. Immediately the alpha chimpanzee lost his drive for dominance and dropped to the bottom of the pecking order. Each of the other chimpanzees moved up one level in the group.

Pecking orders work because each creature feels that he or she is the most important and should be the alpha. This intense feeling drives each creature to compete. The strongest, smartest competitors survive. The alphas mate with each other, thereby producing stronger and more competitive offspring that improve the species with each generation.

Instinctive desires to act kindly, generously, and cooperatively also helped our ancestors survive as they developed rational thought. These instincts balanced their more aggressive desires, softening them so small groups could survive together. Allied with reason and common sense, these kinder instincts make us want to channel our self-advancing instinctive strengths into safe and appropriate actions.

Pecking order feelings are a natural, uncivilized, and unadulterated part of us. They are as valuable as other survival instincts, such as love, hope, joy, anger, envy, hunger, kindness, empathy, loyalty, generosity, and cooperation. We should respect these biological instincts as a source of strength, not hate, fear, or despise them. Untold millions who didn't feel superior were pushed aside and eventually became extinct. Humility may seem more desirable than a raw belief in your own importance, but if your ancestors had been more humble, you probably would not have been born.

Imagine yourself as one of your hairy caveman or cavewoman ancestors 7,000 years ago with your small, hungry band. You haven't eaten all day. You've just killed a bird that's not big enough to satisfy everyone. A large rival is claiming the kill. There are no rules for sharing and no food stamps. He who feels the most important and deserving will demand the largest portion. If you don't stand up for yourself, you starve. Imagine a sense of importance igniting inside you that is ferocious enough to back your rival down. Only that sense of importance will ensure that you eat. Express that feeling by saying something out loud, such as "I will have the most."

Robert Wright's *The Moral Animal* and David Buss's *The Evolution of Desire* summarize how important reaching the top of the pecking order was for our ancestors' survival. It's not wrong that true confidence flows from a biological sense of worth and the raw, unjustified feeling of being entitled to the alpha male or female position. That's the way we are born. It's as simple and inescapable as that.

Confidence Isn't Based on Facts

We'd like to believe confidence is based on our integrity or accomplishments, because then we'd somehow deserve it. Core confidence is untouched by our integrity, accomplishments, or any other facts.

Years ago when my son was 18, he announced on a warm, summer night that he was heading to a rough part of town.

"Dangerous people roam there," I said.

My son—a towering 5' 8" and 150 pounds—said, with swaggering confidence, "I can take care of myself."

Foolishly hoping to overcome his core confidence with fact, I said, "What are you going to do against two or three men with guns?"

His core confidence undeterred, he replied, "I'll outrun them."

I said, with a little swagger myself, "You couldn't outrun me, and I'm a gray-haired, middle-aged man."

"You couldn't begin to keep up with me," he bantered. "I'll race you right now."

"If I win, you stay away from that part of town," I replied.

My thinking brain was objectively analyzing whether or not it should allow me to race and concluded that the odds were strongly against me. Yet, I felt bulletproof.

My son and I lined up in the middle of our street. We agreed that the long crack in the asphalt sixty or so yards away was a good finish line. My wife agreed to start us off.

The following are the expressions of my thinking brain and my core confidence system before and during the race.

Thinking brain: "I can't believe the unmitigated cockiness that is streaming out of you. All logic and facts are against you. You are 45 years old. Your foot speed never exactly lit your high school football cleats on fire, and your son is lean, muscular, and three inches taller. All facts indicate our probability of winning is very low, and the probability is very high that forever more you will be looked down on as a hobbling geezer who can't keep up."

Core confidence: "Mother of God and Holy Saint Joseph, I'm going to explode off this line and blow his doors off."

At this point my core confidence was helping. Instead of feeling tense, I was loose and concentrating and visualizing myself streaking across the finish line way out in front. And as I crouched down for the start, I was pumped.

Thinking brain: "I can't believe that you're smiling. You could end up in the emergency room."

Core confidence: "I'm going to shut this kid down. Tell him he's going to eat my dust!"

Thinking brain: "Bite your tongue. I will not say anything that mean and arrogant."

My wife said, "Ready, get set, go."

At 10 yards:

Thinking brain: "Oh oh. Right off the line your son is ahead by a full yard. You are a hobbling geezer."

Core confidence: "Yes, I'm pumping my arms and starting to gain."

At 20 yards:

Thinking brain: "You're two feet behind."

Core confidence: "Yahoo, I will triumph."

At 30 yards:

Thinking brain: "Your stubby legs are hitting their stride."

Core confidence: "Double Yahoo, I'm winning."

40 yards:

Thinking brain: "You're one foot behind."

Core confidence: "Eat my dust kid."

At 50 yards:

Thinking brain: "It's a dead heat."

Core confidence: "Look out! I'm making the jump to light speed."

Thinking brain: "My goodness, you're crossing the finish line ahead by a full six inches."

Core confidence: "I'm the fastest of all time."

Thinking brain: "You're the luckiest of all time. You should be in the hospital, possibly a mental hospital. Don't gloat, say in a fatherly manner, 'Neither one of us could outrun trouble.'"

Core confidence can do amazing things.

Which Comes First: Confidence or Greatness?

You might argue that celebrities and athletes may feel confident because they have enormous talent and have achieved remarkable success. However, many of them felt confident long before their successes. They seemed to begin with a confident state of mind that helped them succeed.

When Muhammad Ali was a young boy, he often enjoyed gathering dozens of boys around him and addressing them for hours. He also told his father that his name would be on billboards. In 1954, at age 12 and a whopping eighty-nine pounds, Ali first entered the boxing ring to fight three one-minute rounds. Landing a few more punches than his opponent, he was awarded a split decision. He greeted the announcement proclaiming that he would soon be the greatest of all time. As an adult, Ali said, "I am the greatest. I said that even before I knew I was."

At age 10, Alexander the Great bet his father that he could tame and ride a wild horse on which his country's best horseman had given up. He won the bet. The bold personal risks he often took in battle suggest that he believed that he was invincible.

Frank Lloyd Wright's confidence bewildered his friends. With boundless faith in his future success, Wright quit college after one year to become an apprentice to Louis Sullivan, a well-known and revolutionary architect in Chicago. Writer Brendan Gill reported that whenever interviewers described Wright as the greatest living architect, he replied, "What do you mean 'living'?" He thought he was the greatest architect of all time.

Roger Clemens, the major league pitcher, said, "In high school, I was always considered a good pitcher, but I was never considered the best. The thing was, though, I felt I was the best." Jennifer Lopez often said that she was going to be a star long before she was successful. Oscar-winning actor Benicio Del Toro said, "I was born with confidence."

At 14, international self-improvement expert Tony Robbins wrote to major-league sports figures, asking to interview them. He was so talented on camera that a local television station offered him a regular job as a sports interviewer. NBA superstar Patrick Ewing said, "Everybody keeps telling me how surprised they are with what I've done. But I'm telling you honestly that it doesn't surprise me. I knew I could do it."

Because competing for the alpha position was so important to our ancestors' survival, exceptionally intense feelings of strength, worth, and entitlement evolved. These feelings aren't good or bad—they just are. They are hardwired into us. Releasing them while balancing them with kindness and cooperation leads to success.

References

Buss, D. (1994). *The evolution of desire.* New York: Basic Books.

Ferguson, H. (1983). *The edge.* Cleveland: Getting the Edge Company.

Leno, J. (2004). *The actors studio* [Television broadcast]. New York: Bravo.

Pribram, K. H. (1962). Interrelations of psychology and the neurological disciplines. In Koch, S. (Ed.), *Psychology: a study of a science.* New York: McGraw-Hill.

Wright, R. (1994). *The moral animal.* New York: Random House.

CHAPTER 4

Suppression in Everyday Life

"When I'm strong and throwing hard, they aren't going to hit me much. I don't care if they bring a telephone pole up there."

— RON GUIDRY, FORMER MAJOR LEAGUE PITCHER

Our Neolithic ancestors didn't have high intelligence to control core confidence, so a thermostat-like suppressive system evolved in their primitive feeling brains to monitor the intensity of their desires and paralyze them whenever they surged in non-emergency situations.

When our bodies overheat, a regulating system causes us to sweat and keep on sweating, even if the perspiration is soaking through our clothes and embarrassing us. Similarly, when our core confidence becomes too intense for our suppressive systems, it generates insecurity, inadequacy, or self-doubt to shut down the confidence. It does this even when we need confidence, and logic says

47

we should feel it. This suppression occurs unconsciously, much like our kidneys function. The suppressive system isn't capable of speech or thought any more than the kidneys can add or subtract. However, it's helpful to think of the suppressive system as having the intelligence of a 2-year-old child. Beneath our awareness, it becomes alarmed at confidence and reflexively erupts, injecting negativity into us:

- What if I screw this up?
- I should do better.
- If only I could . . . then life would be better.
- I wish I had enough intelligence to . . .
- I am too ordinary.
- If only I were as talented as . . .
- I can't do that.
- I don't think they like me.

It's kind of unfair, isn't it? Though your thinking brain has evolved and could simply decide not to act arrogantly, your suppressive system doesn't care. It still shuts off all but a trickle of your biological belief in yourself, even though you might desperately want that confidence.

What You Get From Suppression

Clients often ask, "Why would one part of my brain consider confidence dangerous and overreact to it?" I ask them if they, or anyone they know, are allergic to pollen. Then I remind them that many people's nasal membranes accurately recognize invisible pollen as harmless particles. They breathe pollen in and out all day long without a reaction. However, other people's nasal membranes overreact, considering pollen dangerous. Most people's suppressive systems can't recognize that core confidence is harmless.

The more intense the confidence, the more deeply we suppress it. When I describe core confidence to clients, they usually think that they already feel the full depth of it. It's just not the case. What we think are our most intense feelings are actually fairly mild. Most of us never realize that our emotional systems have deeper hidden levels containing white-hot core confidence and other strong emotions. Core confidence is a physical feeling, like falling in love: It can make your spine tingle, your toes curl, and your posture straighten.

Unfortunately, the stronger the core confidence, the stronger the corresponding suppressive emotions until you learn to relax that dampening system. Let's look at what happens before you relax your suppressive system.

One of my clients, Tom, reported that he began to feel anxious about work around mid-afternoon every Sunday. Curiously, his anxiety was worse if he had recently been complimented or evaluated positively at work. During three years at his company, he'd never failed to solve a computer problem. He attributed his anxiety to a fear that he would lose his perfect record. Insisting, "I just guess at solutions," he felt like an impostor relentlessly pursued by a plague of compliments.

Actually, he did far more than guess. He listed the five or ten most likely solutions, ranked them in probability of success, and proceeded to try them—an intelligent strategy. Pointing out the wisdom of this strategy made him feel good; a moment later his suppressive system pulled him back into self-criticism.

Tom's unquestionable superiority at work stimulated core confidence so intense that it triggered his suppressive system. I asked him to daydream for a moment that he was superior to his peers, a simple task for most people. Tom couldn't imagine feeling superior, even for a moment. We worked on that for several months using Core Confidence Technique.

As soon as his suppressive system learned that he could feel like a genius, be admired by everyone, and still act in his friendly, unpretentious manner, it relaxed and released his delightful core confidence. Now he walks into work smiling and feeling like a genius.

Suppression in Action

Why would you hold onto something that not only makes you miserable but that you are struggling to discard? You might think you just have a bad habit. Actually, it's your body's way of trying to avoid problems that it perceives will result from acting cocky. B. F. Skinner's widely accepted reward-and-punishment behavior theory has been shown to be valid in thousands of studies.

These studies examined the effects of reward, punishment, or no reward on a variety of different species, including humans, engaged in behaviors that were followed by reward, punishment, or no reward. These studies proved that while an action followed by a reward increases the organism's tendency to repeat that behavior, any behavior followed by punishment or no reward causes the organism to decrease that behavior to the point that it eventually stops.

Here's the tie to suppression: If you were not rewarded for suppression, you would not continue to engage in it. If you continue to create negative thoughts, there must be a hidden reward. Negative thoughts benefit you by relieving your suppressive system's alarm at your core confidence. Your suppressive system doesn't realize you have a rational, thinking brain to stop you from hurting yourself by acting arrogantly or attacking a large animal with only a stick. You don't need your suppressive system anymore, but it doesn't know it doesn't need to make you anxious. But you can teach your suppressive system to relax, and everything will be fine, more than fine. You'll finally feel core confidence. Let's look at Kate.

In my first session with Kate, a 40-year-old saleswoman, the sweat on her fingertips left fleeting spots as she tapped them slowly on the arm of the leather chair she sat in. The muscles in her face strained to hold a composed and confident look. This effort required no thought. It was ingrained, automatic from a lifetime of trying hard to feel sure of herself, comfortable in her own skin, and thinking that if she kept making herself look and act confidently, someday she might actually believe in herself.

Kate's ex-husband had left her deeply in debt and wasn't going to pay child support for their two small children. She said, "I took this 100% commission sales job last month because I need to make a lot more money—at least triple what I made as a low-level manager. My 8-year-old daughter has medical problems and severe learning disabilities. Medicine already absorbs much of my salary. In the future, she's going to need even more help to have any chance at college, and my ex-husband is no help. It's completely up to me. I need confidence to succeed, and I don't have any. I haven't made a sale yet. I'm a failure.

"When I make presentations, my knees are weak, and my stomach is full of butterflies. The good salespeople in my office have the confidence and charisma that make customers believe in them and our products. I'm so tense I can't even fake it. When I call to ask for an appointment, the phone is slipping in my sweaty palm, and I feel sick to my stomach. 'They're busy,' I think. 'They don't want to talk to me, and there's no way I can make them want to give me an appointment.' After an hour, I'm so exhausted that I'm dragging. But I have to make twenty or thirty calls every day."

When I told Kate that her intense core confidence was triggering her suppressive anxieties, she replied, "You're crazy! All my life I've questioned my worth and doubted my decisions. I feel that most people are better than me. Dozens of self-improvement books and two psychologists tried to convince me that I should and could feel good about myself. I'm smart and got good grades in school. Logically, I should feel confident, and sometimes I am, but mostly I feel like I'm just not made of the right stuff."

We discussed why she'd taken the job with no sales experience. She thought she'd taken a desperate gamble, but Kate wasn't a gambler. She took the job because her unconscious core confidence made her feel that she could do it. If she truly never thought she could succeed, she would never have tried for the job.

I asked her if her reasoning for taking the job in the first place was based in thought or in feelings. She replied, "Probably feelings."

We explored this subject. She'd had choices. She'd made the decision to leave a steady, low-level job to pursue sales based on unconscious core confidence. The problem was that she only felt confident for a moment at a time, not long enough to make an impact. Her core confidence often made me smile when it expressed itself in telling me that I was wrong and she was right.

I told her, "Many people are so hypersensitive to core confidence that they trigger a tidal wave of anxiety, depression, or self-loathing before they can feel any confidence. I have clients who can't even say, 'I'm a good person.'"

"How do I make my confidence stronger?" she asked.

"You'd have more luck making yourself taller. Your suppressive system is biologically determined—a written code that can't be overcome. Fortunately, you can persuade it to relax and accept your intense belief in yourself."

I asked Kate to consider that despite having the worst sales month in company history, she'd come to me to spend her last dollar because an unconscious part of her emotional system still believed she could succeed.

I explained Core Confidence Theory over several sessions and described how calls and presentations stimulated several unconscious feelings at once. One primitive system in her feeling brain generated a friendly feeling of wanting to help the customer get the product he or she needed. But no matter how nice a person Kate wanted to be, like all of us, she still wanted to win.

At this point, Kate's emotional brain began to process several things simultaneously and unconsciously. It generated unavoidable instinctive desires to be nice but also to get money from the customer. Her emotional brain also recognized her competitive situation and responded with both a desire to win and core confidence that were so strong that her suppressive system injected paralyzing anxiety. All Kate recognized was that she felt anxious and couldn't perform.

When I described her core confidence and her desire for dominance in the sales situation, Kate was afraid that it would make her act greedy, pushy, and cocky.

I told her that in thirty years, I'd never seen that happen, and it didn't happen with Kate. We continued to work together, doing the visualizations and relaxing her suppressive system, and Kate was eventually able to experience confidence, which brought professional success and personal relief. She was able to care for her children properly and live her life more fully.

These suppressive anxieties can occur in all kinds of situations. Let's look at Steve, who suppressed his confidence in social settings.

Steve is a friendly, active, recently divorced man. An intelligent, successful professional, Steve didn't know why he had always lacked confidence. He wanted to find a new partner, so his difficulty introducing himself to women at night-clubs especially frustrated him. Even though he knew that many women came to dance and meet men, his suppressive system filled his head with thoughts that he wasn't smart, charming, or handsome enough to interest them.

Whenever I invited him to uncover his biological image of himself as a hunk who could sweep women off their feet, Steve chuckled indicating that his core confidence was alive and delighted by this fantasy. Then quickly his suppressive system countered with confusion and denial. He said, "Oh, that's preposterous. I don't even know what to say to women." I continued to discuss how easily he could control his core confidence, and as we practiced Core Confidence Technique, his suppressive system became comfortable with his biological sense of worth. Eventually, it released more confidence than he ever imagined. He radiated strength and poise, and as a result, women were more attracted to him. Steve didn't change physically; he changed mentally and emotionally. It works.

Why is suppression so well developed in some of us? Remember that there is no "normal," only a continuum along which we all fall. Just as some of us have extra-strong arms, so others have an extra-strong suppressive system that over-reacts and creates industrial-strength fears and inadequacies.

Nobody is really safe, though. These drives and suppressive systems produce intense conflicts in almost all of us. They are the source of much daily stress. Conflict is simply part of our nature—it's evolved with us—so even though it can be painful and debilitating, we don't think of it as abnormal. But luckily we can change it.

Reference

Ferguson, H. (1983). *The edge.* Cleveland: Getting the Edge Company.

CHAPTER 5

Facing Your Core Confidence

"For a man to achieve all that is demanded of him, he must regard himself as greater than he is."

— JOHANN WOLFGANG VON GOETHE

Finding confidence depends on getting conscious and unconscious emotional systems to be less afraid of it. This seems counterintuitive, because our entire culture lionizes strength and confidence. Most people have no awareness that core confidence alarms their suppressive system.

One of my clients, Linda, struggled with her self-worth. I suspected suppressive feelings at work and waited for her to provide some clues to her underlying feelings. In the second session, she unconsciously mentioned that she was more successful than her husband. Theoretically, this would stimulate strong feelings of superiority.

I used Confidence Release Technique to convince her suppressive system to relax and uncover more of her hidden feelings. I asked her to visualize her strong love, respect, and appreciation for her husband far outweighing any feelings of superiority she might have. Her suppressive system gradually relaxed and she recognized her fear that if she exuded her enormous confidence, "He couldn't keep up with me, and I would leave him behind."

More reassuring visualizations about the depth of her commitment to her husband further relaxed her suppressive system, and it began to let her feel her core confidence. She began to feel good about herself and even better about him.

Unconsciously we feel that core confidence is as dangerous as nuclear energy. Our suppressive system sees only its intensity, not how strongly we want to channel it productively. Fortunately, desires to be kind, fair, generous, compassionate, and cooperative also had enormous survival value for our ancestors. These inborn feelings make us so strongly want to control our raw confidence that they are more like the useful energy safely contained inside a nuclear reactor rather than lethal radiation.

Controlling Confidence Without Crushing It

Your thinking brain controls your actions. Without confusion, negativity, and other suppressive feelings, the mind becomes clearer, pursuing power and pleasure in many ways, including avoiding self-destructive conceited actions.

People Never Really Lose Control

I believe that people without psychosis or brain damage never *really* lose control of themselves. In my opinion, most of the murderers and violent criminals seen on TV news are likely either psychotic or sociopathic. Their brains function much differently than yours or mine. Just as confidence and anger are biological emotions, so are compassion and love. People who engage in antisocial behavior are missing a healthy dose of compassion and guilt. If you worry about losing control or about hurting other people, your compassion is likely intact.

None of my clients has ever lost control of their core confidence and begun to act arrogantly. At first they worry, but in fact, once they release their core confidence, *they feel more in control than ever.* People who engage in antisocial behavior aren't out of control. They want to act on their impulses more than they want to control them. If you're concerned about losing control, it's likely that you have more than enough motivation to control your actions.

Acting conceited or outwardly showing arrogance isn't necessary in order to enjoy experiencing core confidence. Imagine winning a national prize for one of your talents. Imagine basking in the headlines and the recognition from your friends and family. Can you feel the delightful sense of importance? While feeling that wonderful sensation, do you suddenly want to stop acting kindly and compassionately toward friends and family? Of course not! These emotions aren't mutually exclusive. Confidence and compassion can coexist. You can feel them both at the same time.

Many of my clients at first worriedly say, "Well, I have done some wild things; I could lose control." They report throwing eggs at cars, starting fights, or jumping from a fifty-foot bridge into a lake. Being willing to do wild, risky, or exciting things is different from not being able to stop yourself from doing them. Clarifying this important difference may help you reassure your suppressive system that you can and will "draw the line" when necessary and control your behavior. If you don't control your behavior, it's because you chose not to and not because you actually can't.

Humility Is Often Self-Crushing

One of my clients, Angela, is an unusually intelligent young woman. Most of the time her suppressive system flooded her mind with unfounded criticisms that she was too weird, ugly, and stupid to be successful or attractive. She said, "It feels wrong to feel good about myself. I should strive to feel humble."

I asked, "If core confidence is permanently stamped into your instinctive core, wouldn't it be impossible not to feel it, and therefore, wouldn't it also be impossible to feel only humble?"

She said, "Feeling cocky is a bad thing. I don't think God wants us to feel prideful."

I said, "If you believe that God made your body, then you must believe that He's the one who made survival instincts. Whether or not you like it and whether or not you are conscious of it, your instincts include a raw feeling that you should be at the top of the pecking order. Feeling cocky is part of that instinctive survival emotion."

"Pride is one of the seven deadly sins," Angela said triumphantly.

"If you believe that God made your body, including instinctive feelings that He intended for you to feel, then how can you believe the feelings God put into your body and expects you to experience are bad?"

"Pride is still one of the seven deadly sins," she insisted.

"Don't mistake inescapable inborn confidence for the personal choice of acting cocky or prideful," I said. "That's like saying your hand is bad because you could use it to knock someone's teeth out. Your hand is good and core confidence is good. Deciding to use them in hurtful ways is wrong."

Then I asked, "If core confidence is permanently stamped into your instinctive core, wouldn't it be impossible not to feel it, and therefore, wouldn't it also be impossible to feel only humble?" She agreed. This reassured her thinking brain that feeling confident could hardly be wrong, but her suppressive system was still uneasy.

I said, "Core confidence isn't going away whether or not you approve of it or whether or not it makes sense or feels silly. The desire for a cheeseburger doesn't go away just because you don't have money for one or because it's too high in cholesterol."

Core confidence is important for success and happiness, and as long as you contain it with common sense, it won't cause problems. Suppressing core confidence pushes it out of your awareness, but not out of your emotional system. As a result, you can't see it well enough to control it, so it can express itself arrogantly in your body language without your realizing it. Once you're aware of your core confidence, you can easily decide to control it.

Feel all the core confidence you can. Just guide it with common sense. I'm not suggesting that you take my word for it. It's crucial to evaluate these ideas for yourself. However, in order to make an accurate assessment, you'll have to set suppressive feelings aside.

You can simultaneously feel raw confidence and enough compassion, conscience, or awareness of negative consequences to avoid acting conceited or out of control. As I've mentioned, your independent brain systems clearly enable you to feel all these simultaneously. Can you drink a large soda at the movies and still decide not to relieve your bladder in your seat?

Your thinking brain may be tired of hearing how easily you can control confidence because it learns very quickly. Unfortunately, your feeling brain learns slowly and holds onto its fear of core confidence. I have worked with clients for months, and even though their thinking brains knew they wouldn't act arrogantly, their suppressive systems still paralyzed their confidence.

Persistence Is Important

Bridget was a witty, beautiful, and talented executive. In her 30s, she was frustrated and depressed that she had never been able to attract a suitable mate. She also was cynical about my abilities because two psychologists had not helped her. At the beginning of our sessions, she complained that her time, money, and patience were all running out. However, the fresh pain of being rejected by a recent lover drove her to try once more.

For years Bridget had suppressed her core confidence with feelings of inadequacy and unattractiveness. Convincing this resistant, conservative woman to accept (let alone relish) that she contained raw confidence was difficult. Most of the time, she wouldn't recognize any evidence of her core confidence or her suppressive system until the last few minutes of the session. Often, after sessions, her suppressive system erased our conversation from her memory, so I frequently started the next session from scratch.

Bridget usually became discouraged during our sessions. Repeatedly she was critical of Core Confidence Theory, especially when I illuminated too much of her confidence too fast. Once she stopped sessions for five months, and it appeared as if her suppressive system had defeated us permanently. I wondered if I should have used a more traditional approach. Fortunately, she came back. Occasionally she seemed intrigued when I described her hidden confidence. This was a clue that underneath her despair, her muted and invisible core confidence wanted out. In every session I thought I might be betting her last shot at happiness on the strength of her biological feeling (and I hoped I wasn't mistaken).

Bridget could have been reveling in using her natural beauty and sensuality to captivate men, but though she consciously knew she was beautiful, her suppressive system immersed her in a delusion that she was insecure and somehow not worthy. Although she and an equally attractive girlfriend went to fashionable nightspots to socialize and meet men, she constantly lamented that her friend was prettier because she received much more attention. The friend probably exuded warmer, friendlier, and more sensual cues, while my client suppressed so much of her confidence that she was less fun and certainly less enticing. For example, she said she had an expensive, skin-tight designer dress that she had worn only once because she felt that it made her look like a tramp. When I asked her to describe the dress, she admitted it was cut two inches above the knee with half sleeves and a mock turtleneck. It was tight, but hardly could have made her look like a tramp. But she still *felt* like it made her look like a tramp.

Bridget's only explanation for feeling like a tramp? Her mother disapproved of sexy clothing. Because she had been independent for quite a while, however, her mother's influence should have diminished: her mother had also advised her not to have premarital sex, but she didn't pay any attention to that. Actually, her suppressive system created self-critical feelings to choke off the primitive confidence and sensuality that lure men.

If Bridget had allowed herself to feel confident, she could have controlled any arrogance and exuded a classy, sophisticated air that said, "Yes, I am attractive and sexy, and I love it, but I easily contain it and act in good taste." When I described these bold, confident feelings, she giggled, revealing that her primitive unconscious delighted in the powerful fantasy, but then a moment later her suppressive system bludgeoned her enjoyment with self-criticism and negative thoughts. While grudgingly admitting, "Yes, I am smart, amusing, and clever," she paralyzed her confidence by objecting, "But I have never been charming!" and "I obviously have never been successful with men."

Bridget's suppressive system ran little movies in her mind portraying her as anxious, confused, naive, and desperate, and men as dynamic and desirable. Though seconds earlier she had been giggling at the mention of her enchanting powers, she quickly groaned that she was swirling in a "flushing toilet" of inadequacy.

One evening after she had just begun to release more confidence and sensuality, she attracted more attention at the nightclub than her girlfriend did. But she denied her blossoming vivaciousness by attributing this success to the fact that she was wearing black tights under her skirt. "It wasn't me; it was the tights." Her suppressive thoughts were unnecessary because she would have consciously controlled her core confidence. She knew conceit ruined relationships. The more she showed her suppressive system that she would consciously contain her confidence, the more it let her feel attractive and sensual. Her increased confidence helped her attract and contend with men, and she felt more confident and comfortable in social situations in general. In business settings, she felt more talented and capable and acted with more power and assertiveness. She applied for and got a senior management position with a larger corporation, doubling her salary in only a couple of years.

I'd like to say this story had an even happier ending, but outcomes aren't always cut and dry dried. Being aware of core confidence isn't enough. Realizing you need to relax your suppressive system so you can enjoy your emotions isn't enough. Your suppressive system is a network of emotions with the intelligence of a 2-year-old. It may take repeated visualizations in order to believe in yourself. You must do the visualizations for as long as it takes.

Bridget stopped therapy even though her suppressive system still hadn't fully allowed her to believe that she was attractive to men. In fact, she may have stopped therapy because we were starting to uncover intense feelings that she could easily lure and control men. Her suppressive system was just too uncomfortable to let her enjoy feeling *that* sensual and desirable. No matter how I presented the reassuring visualization exercises, she resisted them. She complained that she was always busy and that it was difficult and uncomfortable for her to visualize. Her suppressive system manufactured these feelings to prevent her from uncovering the confidence she wanted. Suppressive systems are tricky. They may be comfortable with you feeling confident in one area of your life, such as business, but not in another, such as dating. If you have trouble visualizing, your suppressive system is reacting strongly. You must persuade your suppressive system to relax. Though your suppressive system is a major obstacle to confidence, it just needs reassurance.

Realize you do have control. You can always act sensibly and diplomatically.

CHAPTER 6

Uncovering Your Confidence and Feeling Your Magic

"Vanity is one of the great comforts of life."

— BENJAMIN FRANKLIN

You may think, "OK, instinctive confidence makes sense, and I'm sure I can control it. So why doesn't it come?" Though suppression is a very simple concept, it's not usually simple to undo. Your thinking brain may know that you can control your raw confidence, but your suppressive system isn't logical, barely understands language, certainly can't listen to reason, and is programmed to protect your family and friends from your core confidence as long as you live. However, your suppressive system *does* respond to feelings and pictures. You need to let it watch as you vividly imagine yourself *feeling* core confidence while you also *feel* that you want to control it.

For most people, this process is not a one-day magic cure. Your suppressive system is a primitive system and learns to relax slowly. However, there is good news: Every time you show your suppressive system how harmless raw confidence actually is, it relaxes a bit and injects less anxiety the next time your core confidence surges. Finally, your inborn confidence can surface and make you feel as if you're a foot taller, twice as smart, and three times as good-looking.

This chapter and the next two present a number of exercises that can make your suppressive system more comfortable with your core confidence. Your suppressive system will start to respect (instead of being alarmed by) the sense of worth and importance inside you. You don't need to look for words to say, thoughts to think, or formulas to follow. Whenever you lack confidence or think, "How do I release my biological belief in myself?" sit back, relax, and enjoy the simple visualization exercises in this program.

> Your suppressive system triggers or relaxes without your conscious direction, so you might as well take a vacation from intellectually trying to hurry it along. Rather than trying to force more confidence, loosen up and relish recognizing, respecting, and loving your core confidence.

The 4 Rs: Recognize, Respect, Reassure, Release

Each time you *recognize* your core confidence, *respect* it, and *reassure* yourself that you can control it, your suppressive system relaxes its paralyzing anxiety and self-criticism. You gradually desensitize your suppressive system, and it *releases* an even more powerful belief in yourself. This increased flow of confidence sharpens and energizes your conscious mind, which responds, "Oh, this feels good. I need to release even more of this." This positive feeling further persuades your suppressive system that it can safely release even stronger confidence. The more you reassure your suppressive system, the more it relaxes and the more primordial confidence it releases. This gentle yet powerful self-reinforcing cycle—*recognizing, respecting, reassuring, releasing*—is the path toward having confidence beyond measure.

The 4 Rs Program

- *Recognize* the deep primitive feelings that generate confidence.
- *Respect* them as your major source of strength and happiness.
- *Reassure* your suppressive system that you want to and will act appropriately.
- Wait for your suppressive system to *release* its iron grip.

This approach uses simple, proven techniques such as modeling, systematic desensitization, and creative visualization. All of the exercises promote feeling confident, comfortable, and in control at all times. All of these techniques encourage you to *feel* really good about yourself, but to *act* sensibly.

Desensitization

Systematic desensitization is a well-proven psychological technique for making the emotional system more comfortable with anything it finds alarming or frightening. First, you present a mild form of the alarming stimulus and wait for your feeling brain to recognize that it's harmless. When your feeling brain gets comfortable with this stimulus, you then systematically present increasingly intense levels of stimuli, waiting for your feeling brain to relax before intensifying the stimulus again. For example, if you wanted to be less fearful of snakes, I might first have you look through a window into a room containing a snake in a glass cage. Even though your thinking brain would know that the snake wasn't a threat, your feeling brain would probably still be alarmed. I'd have you watch the snake until your feeling brain gradually learned that the snake couldn't hurt you and finally let you relax.

This process might take two or twenty minutes, depending on your emotional system's initial fear level. After you relaxed, I'd gradually move the caged snake closer and closer, at each point waiting for your feeling brain to again learn that you were safe. Eventually, your feeling brain would learn that you could even safely hold the snake. In the chapters that follow, we'll use this well-researched and widely accepted desensitization program to teach your suppressive system to be comfortable with your instinctive core confidence and to stop paralyzing it with insecurity.

I will guide you through statements and daydream-like visualizations that will stimulate your feeling brain to generate core confidence. Your suppressive system will learn that as you enjoy this raw, satisfying confidence, your compassion and common sense will easily allow you to channel your confidence safely. I will present visualizations that gradually stimulate increasing core confidence in order to invite your suppressive system to warm up to confidence instead of triggering suppressive action. If you find yourself bored, confused, anxious, or distracted during the exercises, you may have visualized a level of confidence that triggered your suppressive system. If so, back down to a less intense visualization.

Modeling

Humans learn a tremendous amount from simply watching others and imitating them. We automatically create internal models of what we see others do, and then we unconsciously follow these models. Whenever my father returned from spending a few days in the South, he unconsciously picked up the accent. If you've ever observed children, you see the power and pervasiveness of their imitative abilities from a very young age. Years ago, I noticed my sister's young children frequently yelling "sit on it" at each other. Later that evening, I watched a new TV show called *Happy Days* and its cool character Fonzie expressing his favorite phrase, "Sit on it!" The children had quickly copied his behavior. Countless similar examples demonstrate that what we see influences our behavior. Advertising is a perfect example. Corporations spend billions of dollars on TV commercials to depict people using their product and expressing delight. They know you will internalize that model and that repeated exposures render you ever more likely to eventually reach for their product.

This chapter will show you how to relax your suppressive system by watching other people successfully release core confidence. More importantly, you will learn to create your own visualized mental models of yourself safely and successfully releasing your core confidence without hurting anyone.

Creative Visualization

Thirty years ago, Dr. Douglas Denny and I published three research studies showing that watching people handle snakes (visual models) helped people who had a phobia of snakes feel less afraid. Those who imagined themselves handling snakes also reduced their fear. Today this psychological tool originally used by professionals is a household word: "creative visualization."

Visualization is one of the most effective tools for change, and it is used in many therapeutic techniques. Your mind creates vivid mental images (models) that your unconscious automatically follows, much as it follows models in the real world. These images can even cause your body to respond physiologically. For example, right now think about holding a freshly cut lemon wedge in the palm of your hand. See its vivid yellow peel and imagine the citrus smell. Now, imagine you are plunging your teeth deep into the lemon and sucking the juice over your lips and tongue. Most people will pucker and salivate, even though no lemon is present. Similarly, simply imagining sexual scenes will arouse your body.

Visualizing mental models for your feeling brain to follow is so effective that most world-class athletes spend considerable time imagining themselves performing perfectly. Before every dive, Olympic-champion diver Greg Louganis visualized his movements until he could see and "feel" they were perfect. Superstar golfer Jack Nicklaus said, "I never hit a shot, not even in practice, without having a very sharp, in-focus picture of it in my head."

In his book *Peak Performance*, Charles Garfield reported several studies showing the benefits of visualization training. The most interesting was a 1976 Soviet study comparing the performance of four groups of world-class athletes after mental training (primarily visualization and relaxation). The first group received 100% physical training. The second, third, and fourth groups spent, respectively, twenty-five percent, fifty percent, and seventy-five percent of their training time in mental training. The more mental training a group received, the more its actual performance improved, even though members had received less physical training.

Research also demonstrates that visualizing the number of immune cells in your body increasing or decreasing actually can cause the quantity to increase or decrease. Great leaders have clear images of what they want, and they use these images to inspire others. Salespeople who visualize their last successful sale before making a sales presentation sell more.

Many successful people have used visualization to achieve success. From the time she was a little girl, Marilyn Monroe imagined herself as an incredibly sexy, sensual, seductive woman. Andrew Carnegie, Henry Ford, Wilbur Wright, William J. Kaiser, and many other extremely successful people considered visualization a key factor in their success. Roger Bannister repeatedly visualized himself as the first man to break the four-minute mile barrier.

Unfortunately, we also respond to negative images. Karl Wallenda, of the world-famous Flying Wallendas' high-wire act, may have unconsciously followed a negative internal model to tragedy. His wife reported that during the many decades that he walked the high wire, he had never thought about falling. Wallenda began to think about falling, for the first time, a month before he and several family members fell to their deaths.

Remember, your emotional system understands the pictures and feelings that you vividly imagine much better than language. To release your belief in yourself, you will create images of yourself brimming with raw confidence, easily keeping it under control, and channeling it into appropriate and successful actions. You will frequently bathe your suppressive system in these healthy mental images. Read on for how to get started and hints for success.

Visualize from Inside Your Body

Because your suppressive system responds more to vivid images—which trigger vivid feelings—than it does to intellectual thoughts, visualize as clearly as you can. Begin with a visualization with which your suppressive system is comfortable. As your suppressive system adjusts to your core confidence, it will allow you to visualize scenes that stimulate progressively more intense feelings. I believe that there are four main levels of visualization. From mildest to most intensely stimulating they are as follows:

Level 1: Imagine watching someone across the room as they feel and act confidently. This level stimulates the least core confidence and therefore alarms your suppressive system the least.

Level 2: Picture yourself across the room feeling and acting confidently.

Level 3: Visualize what it feels like for another person to be inside their body looking out through their eyes at the others in the scene and feeling confidence rising inside them as they speak and act. (Some may find Level 3 easier to visualize than Level 2.)

Level 4: Imagining yourself actually inside your body looking out through your eyes and feeling confidence rising inside you.

Start at the level that feels comfortable. Begin each level by visualizing mildly confident feelings and actions. For example, at Level 1, you might picture someone feeling good about herself while saying hello to a stranger.

As your suppressive system becomes more comfortable with each level, it will gradually let you imagine confident feelings and actions as progressively more intense physical or sensuous experiences in your body. For example, you might begin by imagining another person smiling optimistically and feeling good about herself in a job interview and then progress to feeling your chest expand with confidence as you sit in your own job interview.

When you're visualizing yourself feeling deeper confidence, remember that deeper levels of confidence include stronger physical sensations. For example, visualizing yourself confidently giving a reserved, formal speech to five people would desensitize your suppressive system. Visualizing yourself giving a lively, uninhibited speech to 1,000 people would stimulate more intense confidence and help your suppressive system become comfortable with it. Uncovering the deepest level of confidence would involve visualizing yourself speaking to 1,000 people while feeling your body filled with powerful physical feelings, such as excitement coursing through your body, your chest expanding, your eyes "owning" the room, your gestures powerful and expressive, your body standing taller, and in general feeling invincible, on top of the world. I sometimes refer to these physical sensations as fanny-wriggling, toe-curling confidence.

Steps to Successful Visualization

1. Choose a goal.
2. Relax deeply to focus your attention.
3. Visualize yourself performing perfectly. Include movements, such as hand gestures, and physical sensations, such as warm, tingly, pleasurable feelings.
4. Focus on your goal, effortlessly, as if in a pleasant daydream. Don't try to create images. Let them come. Detailed images will be presented later.

For additional information about visualization, read Shakti Gawain's *Creative Visualization* (an excellent step-by-step guide to visualization) and Maxwell Maltz's *Psycho-Cybernetics.*

Moving Ahead Too Quickly Can Alarm Your Suppressive System

Eager to make progress, many people immediately jump to the advanced exercises. Others sometimes think that these exercises are paced for emotionally fragile people and want to rush through them in a week. Moving too quickly can backfire by sensitizing your suppressive system and causing it to overreact. The overreaction may feel like a mere loss of interest or the usual self-doubt or debilitating tension, confusion, or other negative feelings.

Don't Underestimate the Sensitivity of Your Suppressive System.

Jerry, a tall, muscular, 30-year-old male client with a thick, closely cropped beard, had the rugged look of a barroom bouncer, yet he felt anxious and inadequate with women. I asked him to imagine that he felt confident and attractive. Even this small amount of confidence triggered his suppressive system, which then immediately filled him with insecurity. He stoically gave no sign of these feelings, so I intensified the imagery to stimulate even more core confidence by inviting him to imagine he was at a party and that beautiful women were flocking around him. His suppressive system immediately injected so much anxiety that he felt sick and dizzy and couldn't continue the exercise.

I've never seen anyone overcome his suppressive system. It's the Godzilla of your mind. The urge to overcome your suppressive system will lead you to failure. I have seen clients push too hard and sensitize their suppressive systems into paralyzing them with so much confusion, frustration, and hopelessness that they were never able to complete the exercises and never understood why. Battling your suppressive system will distract you from enjoying the slower, but far more successful, strategy of lulling it to sleep.

Be careful. This intellectual warning probably will not stop other self-driving systems in your feeling brain from generating an urge to push ahead. (Chapter Eight, "Meet Your Drill Sergeant," illuminates this hidden problem and offers a comprehensive approach to stopping it.)

In general you let your feeling systems watch as you imagine your desire to push yourself causes you to feel fatigue and frustration. Then you imagine the gradual, no pressure approach leading you to success. Fortunately, even if this visualization fails to stop your drill sergeant, your thinking brain still has control of your actions and can decide to proceed at a sensible pace.

You may be tempted to keep pushing to conquer your suppressive feelings—such as anxiety, confusion, and self-doubt—in a demanding, tough-minded strategy. Unfortunately, this strategy is as effective as attempting to ram your head through a stone wall.

When to Advance and When to Retreat

Enjoy each exercise at least four or five times before advancing.

Once you are regularly feeling a strong, physical experience of core confidence during an exercise, you may be ready to advance to the next exercise. If the next exercise stimulates suppressive feelings, such as confusion or boredom, that prevent you from feeling confident, you probably need to return to the previous exercise for a while. Stay with the previous exercise until you feel no suppressive emotions while doing the visualizations. Move to the next level only after you feel physically relaxed, comfortable, and really good about yourself. At the next level, continue the more advanced exercises until your confidence feels physically pleasurable.

At first, you may not feel even a glimmer of confidence during the exercises, even if you do them for a week or longer. If so, look for encouraging signs that your suppressive system is relaxing, such as feeling more comfortable during the exercises or experiencing a reduction in anxiety, confusion, self-criticism, or other negative feelings. Take heart in this progress.

We want to continuously surround your suppressive system with an atmosphere of complete comfort about your control, common sense, and compassion for others. Once you are familiar with these exercises, you can stimulate these reassuring feelings whenever you wish, even if you don't have the book to follow. If you only have a few moments, focus on one or two key reassuring statements, such as "I'm going to act sensibly, so it's perfectly safe for me to feel really good about myself." Don't say these statements as affirmations to convince yourself. Say them and wait to see if your suppressive system relaxes and releases raw confidence.

Daydreams Uncover Core Confidence

We don't have to work at daydreams. They seem to wander along, rolling out such pleasant thoughts that we often steal time during other activities to enjoy them. Your core confidence visualizations should feel just that natural and pleasurable.

Begin daydreaming about your deep belief in yourself by feeling certain that you'll act sensibly. Just open your mind to the fantasy and let your unconscious core confidence systems create an image of you feeling confident in an important setting. Enjoy letting your confidence systems effortlessly move the daydream along into deeper, more intense, and more pleasurable images of you feeling valuable and important. If your suppressive system injects anxiety, boredom, or other distractions, recognize them as suppressive and in order to return to your comfortable state, again reassure your suppressive system with images of you preferring to act sensibly. It's helpful to think of this as taking your suppressive system by the hand and introducing it to progressively deeper and stronger levels of your core confidence.

The first time one of my clients felt a glimmer of raw confidence, she believed she was alienating everyone. I recommended that she check to see whether she had caused any terrible problems or whether her confidence had actually been harmless. I asked her to do these "harmlessness checks" whenever she worried that her confidence might be a problem. These checks helped her learn that feeling intense confidence did absolutely no damage and was quite empowering. She stopped choking it off with self-criticism and channeled it toward finding a boyfriend. (Her newfound poise attracted, as she put it, a "real hunk.")

Whenever you feel a moment of core confidence, help your suppressive system warm up to it by checking that it didn't do any damage. Let both your thinking and feeling brains note whether your raw confidence caused any serious losses or injuries or if it was completely harmless. Notice if anyone's arms or legs have been blown off. Look for bloodstains on your clothing and furniture. Count all your fingers and toes. Note if the house is still standing. Did anyone even notice your feelings? This may seem ridiculous, but remember, your suppressive system isn't logical or intelligent, doesn't learn easily, and has enormously exaggerated fantasies of your power. If your suppressive system has a tight grip, you may find that you need to play with this exercise often.

We're going to show your suppressive system reassuring images again and again until it finally embraces them. Later exercises will make your suppressive system comfortable with progressively deeper and more intense levels of core confidence.

Visualize the images as often as you comfortably can. Enjoy them as you eat, walk, or shower. Even though your thinking brain may become comfortable with the concepts in one listening (and you think that you've learned all you can and should move on), your slow-learning suppressive system will likely need much more exposure before it will release your core confidence. Most likely you won't recognize this because your suppressive system, like most of your feeling brain, functions completely out of your awareness. It doesn't tell you, "I'm still paralyzing your core confidence." It works invisibly, as your kidneys do. You only know your kidneys are working because you can feel your bladder is full. Similarly, you only know your suppressive system is working when you feel the distraction, confusion, inadequacy, or self-criticism that it generates to paralyze your core confidence. The more you play with these exercises, the more quickly you will recognize your suppressive thoughts. Eventually, you'll recognize them as they're happening: "Oh, here I am covering up my confidence with doubt and self-criticism again."

Confidence Doesn't Have to Be Factual

Core confidence can be completely unrealistic but still empower you and maximize your performance. When you face great challenges, you don't have to actually *be* the best, strongest, or smartest. You only have to *feel* that you're better, faster, smarter, stronger, and more creative. You don't have to *be* superhuman. You only need to *feel* superhuman.

Judging whether or not your skill or intelligence justifies your confidence distracts you and disturbs your performance. Your suppressive system may be distorting your judgment. Concentrate on opening up to your unshakable belief in yourself. (Strong emotional interest rivets our attention on something. So, when I suggest that you concentrate, that really means let yourself get interested.) Because so few people are empowered by their core confidence, if you can feel your biological belief in yourself, you probably will sweep beyond even more talented and more experienced competitors.

Notice and take satisfaction in small increases in confident feelings or actions, such as feeling less nervous or speaking up more easily. Let go of any frustrating demand to gain confidence immediately. Uncovering raw confidence gradually is far better than feeling insecure forever. Avoid criticizing yourself or demanding quicker success. Retake the Confidence Suppression Test and the Baseline Confidence Measure in Chapter 2 to remind yourself that you are making progress.

I've never had a client who didn't encounter some of the following problems. These snags are hard to spot and even harder to understand. Frequently, they are created and hidden by your suppressive system. I can help clients recognize and resolve them, but I can't be there to point them out as they happen to you. You will have to notice and diagnose them. This will take attention and persistence. When you feel insecure, stuck, or bored, reread this section.

Suppressive Avoidance

Suppressive systems can subtly resist releasing confidence by distracting you from these exercises with fatigue, criticism, hopelessness, procrastination, and other suppressive tricks. If you find these exercises aren't interesting, if you feel they aren't enough, or if you think you just don't have time to do them, your suppressive system is probably responsible. Watch out for these!

If the exercises make you feel silly or stuck, recognize this as suppression and reread this chapter.

You may feel so busy or pressured to produce results that you can't justify taking time to do these exercises, even though you know that gaining a deep belief in yourself would make you enormously more successful at dating, selling, interviewing, negotiating, and almost anything else. Many of my clients took four years out of their lives to get a college education, yet most, at the beginning, worried that they didn't have time for these exercises. Taking ten minutes a day to gain confidence could contribute enormously to your success and happiness. That said, you have to go about it the right way. Forcing yourself to do these exercises won't help.

Whenever clients say to me, "I'll work on that," I cringe, because I know framing it as "working" is often a progress killer. Your feeling brain doesn't like to be pushed or pressured, and it usually doesn't like to work. If you approach this as a job to be accomplished, no matter how much your thinking brain wants confidence, your emotional system will tense up and drag its feet. It will make you feel tight and pressured. You will push and struggle. It won't be fun, and you won't get much out of it. You've probably already pushed and tried quite a bit, and I suspect it hasn't worked any better for you than it did for me or my clients. Often your suppressive system gets you pushing and struggling to change because pushing and struggling tie you in an emotional knot and help prevent your immense core confidence from automatically surfacing.

You will uncover more confidence if you pretend you are secretly indulging in a daydream. Relax and bring up a pleasant visualization that you are magic and can do anything, the same way you'd visualize yourself on vacation or alone with the love of your life. Just sit and wait for the pleasant feelings to start bubbling up.

Play, Don't Push.

Don't say the statements in the visualizations persuasively, the way most people say affirmations. Affirmations don't affect your suppressive system. Some of the statements in the exercises may sound like affirmations, but affirmations are directed by your thinking brain. These statements should be emotional invitations to let unconscious feelings surface. You shouldn't be trying to convince yourself that you're wonderful. Your suppressive system won't buy in and it'll tie you in a knot. It will work about as well as writing the feelings on paper and then trying to push the paper into your brain through your nose. Wanting, trying, and struggling are not the same thing as waiting for your suppressive system to relax and release your inborn belief in yourself.

The same goes for forcing yourself to do these exercises when you don't want to. Forcing yourself will create emotional resistance, undermining your effort and teaching your emotional system to hate these exercises. That's disaster. It's better to wait until you feel eager or at least interested in playing with the exercises. You wouldn't force yourself to daydream about vacation. Don't force yourself to daydream about feeling confident either. This should feel good.

Thinking Instead of Feeling Is a Dead End

You need to move beyond thinking, way past: "I think I can," to actually *feel in your body* a surging, mindless, reasonless faith in your own strength, genius, and attractiveness. When fully uncovered, this feeling should cause welcome sensory responses in your body, such as a pleasurable rush that makes your toes curl. This raw biological feeling should also spur thoughts such as "I am magic" and "no one can stop me." Imagine how you might feel if you won the lottery.

Thinking about your insecurities is one of the most common and difficult-to-recognize suppressive tricks. Thinking pulls you away from feeling. Thousands of times I have guided clients through visualizations that invite them to feel delicious core confidence, only to have them subtly move away from focusing on *feeling* confident to *thinking* about related topics or specific self-doubts or other negative feelings. I ask them to step back from these thoughts and replay how they came to mind. If you find this happening to you during the visualizations, check to see if you're thinking instead of actually feeling delicious core confidence. If you are, recognize this thinking as suppression, step back, and soak in more reassurance that nothing bad will happen if you allow yourself to feel confident. (Of course, you can't actually "soak in" reassuring feelings. All you can do is invite yourself to picture them so that your suppressive system can also feel them. However, the symbolic image of soaking reassurance into your emotional system lends a feeling of power and action to the process.)

Spine-Tingling Confidence Beyond Anything You've Ever Felt

When I describe deep-level core confidence, clients often say, "I have felt that." If they keep looking deeper, they usually find stronger, more empowering confidence and realize that their suppressive system had been limiting them to a memory of mildly confident feelings and perceiving them as the deepest level possible. Don't let your suppressive system trick you into believing that what you've felt in the past is all you can feel.

Remember, you can control the big tip-offs that you feel cocky, such as boasting and swaggering. People will read your remaining, more subtle body language, such as smiling and erect posture, as energy, enthusiasm, and feeling good about yourself. Healthy people are excited by and attracted to people who feel good about themselves.

Clients often say, "I don't want all of my suppression to go away." They mistakenly think that if all of their suppression went away, they would act conceited. You do want all your suppression to go away because you can easily decide to act sensibly. Suppression is only paralyzing you.

Progress can be slower and more frustrating than you want it to be, sometimes even maddeningly slow. Sometimes people can't feel much happening in their bodies. Remember, your suppressive system resets its thermostat gradually in response to visualizations of safely feeling confident. This happens beneath your awareness, as springtime gradually emerges from a long, cold winter. At first, you wait for a brief glimpse of confidence like you wait for a warm day in early spring that is always followed by bursts of cold days. Don't give up. Persist. Visualizations are free and easy.

What to Do When Insecurity Strikes

As you go through your normal day, anxiety or self-doubt may surge through you. Many times this happens just when you're about to start a project, introduce yourself, present your ideas, or strike up a conversation.

This insecurity usually just hits you, and it seems so foreign to think that an intense belief in yourself (one you can't even feel consciously) actually triggers your invisible suppressive system to generate that insecurity. Countless everyday events stimulate our instinctive confidence systems to generate energizing grandiose feelings in all of us. We either enjoy and channel this confidence or tie ourselves into a knot to suppress it.

When suppression strikes and you fear you will falter in a situation, use the following three-step action plan:

1. recognize insecurity as suppression
2. feel energized by your anger at being suppressed, and
3. "soak" reassurance into your suppressive system to make it relax.

Recognize self-doubts as suppression caused by intensifying core confidence. Say something to yourself, such as "These self-doubts must be suppressive. Somewhere, inside me, my confidence must be surging and triggering my suppressive system." The more you do these exercises, the more quickly you'll recognize that insecurity is likely suppression and take these steps to stop it.

The burst of energy that comes with anger can help you contend with suppression. Healthy irritation or anger was genetically programmed into your body to make you want to conquer pain and problems. Suppression, like any other painful problem, instinctively makes you feel healthy anger. For example, you might feel, "This miserable suppression makes me mad!"

Natural, healthy anger is different than uncomfortable, frustrated, suppressed anger. Frustrated anger feels terrible. It makes people want to say, "This suppression is driving me nuts." Healthy anger feels energizing and empowering. For example, "I don't like this suppression; I'm going to stop it." This energizing irritation or anger will make you eager for the third step: "soaking" lots of reassurance into your suppressive system to make it relax and stop paralyzing your confidence.

Exactly what kind of reassuring feelings should you "soak" in? The best you can do is to guess at the feeling triggering the suppression and then customize your reassurance to it. For example, if you feel insecure walking into a party or meeting that you have no logical reason to feel insecure about, you might ask yourself, "Most social situations stimulate instinctive pecking-order feelings of value and importance to energize me to gain the alpha position. Am I unconsciously worried that I'm feeling so important that I'll start acting conceited?" If this scenario seems accurate, you can "soak" in reassuring images of you wanting to say something conceited but simultaneously even more strongly wanting to act friendly and deciding to speak unpretentiously. Then begin the three-step action plan:

The Three-Step Action Plan
Step One: Recognize Insecurity as Suppression

Unfortunately, most of us believe that insecurities and feelings of inadequacy are part of our central core, our deepest feelings. Once you've begun doing the exercises, you will get better and better at recognizing suppression when it takes hold. The exercises will build an accurate picture of your central core as full of an unquestioned belief in yourself. When you compare your insecurities against this clear sense of your instinctive confident self, your insecurities won't fit with this confident picture of you, and you'll realize that your suppressive system fabricated them. The more you do these exercises, the more quickly you'll make the connection that insecurity is actually suppression and take steps to stop it.

Whenever you feel insecure:

- Automatically think: "This insecurity isn't my core feeling. Where is my instinctive core confidence? This insecurity must be paralyzing it."

- Notice the absence of the confidence that should be inside you and the presence of the suppressive feelings that shouldn't be inside you.
- Conclude that you're very likely suppressing raw confidence.

Step Two: Let Your Natural Anger Energize You

My clients are often angry about being limited by these insecurities instead of being able to feel confident and relish living moments of their lives productively. Use that anger to get your suppressive system out of the way. This step briefly addresses frustrated anger. If you're feeling frustrated, your mobilizing anger is likely paralyzed by suppressive frustration. This is often distressing and robs you of your energy to take productive, appropriate action to resolve the problem. You may want to spend time on warming your suppressive system up to your healthy anger in the same way these exercises warm it up to your core confidence. Unsuppressed healthy anger is more comfortable than anger suppressed with distressing frustration or the feeling of being victimized. It's much easier to control, contain, and channel anger into moral, ethical, and legal actions that create acceptable resolutions to anger-producing problems or situations. I am not encouraging or endorsing anyone to hurt or damage any person, animal, or property. Removing suppressive feelings of frustration or of being victimized helps us recognize anger clearly and realize that we are not entitled to hurt because we are angry. Anyone with persistent feelings of rage should see a mental health professional to relieve these painful emotions.

- Visualize yourself feeling certain that you'll act sensibly while you also notice uncovering and accepting progressively deeper anger.
- Don't try to make yourself angry. Notice how much you don't like insecurity making you uncomfortable and diminishing your success. This should automatically stimulate energizing anger.
- Wait for the anger to surface effortlessly. Making statements such as "I'm fed up with this suppressive insecurity; I'm going to get comfortable with my core confidence," may help focus your feelings and invite your anger to surface. Energizing irritation or anger will make you eager for the third step: soaking in reassurance into your suppressive system to make it relax and stop paralyzing your confidence.
- *Accept that you can't make your suppressive system stop. That's impossible.* The best you can do is to flood your suppressive system with a reassuring

feeling of how strongly you want to control both your anger and your core confidence. Then keep on reassuring it until it finally learns to relax and stops paralyzing your confidence.

Step Three: Soak Reassuring Feelings into Your Suppressive System

When insecurity strikes you, reassuring your suppressive system that you can control your actions will make it relax and stop injecting insecurity into you. So you need to be able to summon reassuring feelings quickly.

You might think, "But I'm not worried that I would lose control, and I already know that I don't want to act conceited."

Your thinking brain knows that, but your suppressive system doesn't know that. You need to immerse your suppressive system not just in the thought but also in the physical feeling that it's completely safe to feel your core confidence because you most want to act sensibly.

The Reassuring Feeling of Control

Feelings are surprisingly foreign to many people. Their emotional systems are uncharted territory. Many people think that they are feeling when actually they are thinking about feeling. Clients often say, "I know intellectually that I can control my actions, but I don't know how to *feel* that I'm under control or how to *feel* that raw confidence is harmless. How do I get myself to *feel* my own sense of control rather than just understand intellectually it is there?"

Getting to know this feeling involves being curious enough to "explore feeling until you experience feeling." At first, you may be mostly thinking and visualizing without much feeling. But if you hang in here with me, groping around in the dark, so to speak, eventually we'll stumble onto more feeling. After stumbling around for a while, clients often experience a breakthrough of sorts and exclaim, "Oh, now I understand the feeling of control that you're talking about." One of my clients described it as "a feeling of certainty," that is, she felt certain that she would act sensibly.

Here's an example of really feeling in control: Imagine yourself walking up to a bank teller who has tall stacks of twenty-dollar bills on her counter. Your honesty or the security cameras ensure that you will decide not to steal the money. Still, some part of your survival instincts should be generating a desire to grab a couple of those thick stacks and run out the door. You *know* that you're not going to reach for the money, but you should also be able to sense a less intellectual and more primitive *feeling* process in your body that your arm is not reaching for the money, and you're not going to reach for it. That's a feeling of control.

Wait for tiny flickers of this feeling of control. Waiting is important. Accept that it will take time to reassure your suppressive system and look forward to doing lots of it.

Remember Kate from Chapter 4, who felt anxious in her new sales job? For several weeks she "soaked in" reassuring visualizations that she could easily control her core confidence while making sales presentations. Yet, she uncovered little core confidence. She was disappointed, frustrated, and feeling a little desperate. I asked her if she was focusing on the "active ingredient," the physical feeling in her body that she was strongly committed to acting sensibly no matter how intensely confident she began to feel. She assured me that she was.

To make sure, I took her through one of the visualizations and asked her to describe exactly what she was experiencing. She reported feeling that she needed and wanted confidence to happen "right now." She was a quick, clear-thinking person, and without realizing it, she was actually thinking about feeling rather than experiencing physical sensations in her body. For starters, she was picturing herself across the room rather than experiencing being inside her body, looking out through her eyes and feeling the emotional sensations in her body.

Kate's habit of substituting thoughts about reassuring feelings for the feelings themselves led me to fine-tune the reassuring visualizations in the Confidence Release Technique to stimulate more physical sensations. I asked her to visualize herself inside her body, looking out through her eyes and seeing a symbolic, friendly, common-sense-and-compassion path in front of her. I asked her to imagine that her common sense and all her kind and friendly feelings, including her desire to have warm, friendly relationships with people, were in the right side of her body. Next, I asked her to visualize friends and loved ones standing along the friendly path and to feel in her body her desire to be loved and respected by them. She felt that in order to keep her friends' and family's respect and love, she would need to (and strongly wanted to) act kindly and unpretentiously toward them. I asked her to picture these people smiling and glad to see her. She experienced physical sensations of wanting to walk down this path and emotionally connect with these people. These feelings were so strong that even if she felt smarter, stronger, and more popular, she also felt absolutely committed to acting friendly and unpretentiously toward them.

Kate's suppressive system didn't say to her, "Oh, I'm feeling much more comfortable about your ability to control your core confidence." But she enjoyed this "daydream" several times a day and within a few days she experienced brief surges of feeling really good about herself. Within a few months, she was feeling smart, strong, and bullet-proof during sales presentations. When customers doubted her products and rejected her proposals, she smiled and respectfully acknowledged their questions, bouncing back eager to explore their objections and meet them with the most persuasive response possible.

You won't consciously notice feelings of control soothing your suppressive system either. You can't see your suppressive system paralyze you, and you can't see or feel it relax. You also can't see or feel the reassurance you "soak" in relaxing it. You've got to blindly "soak" reassurance into your suppressive system, and you have to soak it in again and again—many times without any noticeable effect. It takes time for the reassurance to stick, to sink in. You need to wait until your suppressive system relaxes and uncovers a glimmer of raw confidence. That glimmer will manifest as a bodily sensation, a body feeling. That is the feeling you're looking for. At times you may wait while trembling with anxiety or sweating with self-doubt as you face presentations, job interviews, and other challenges. At these times it may seem as though there is nothing inside you but weakness, insecurity, and inadequacy. At these moments you may feel that Core Confidence Theory is baloney or that you're the exception, the one who was born without core confidence.

Persist, bet on yourself. Look for small increases in confidence, such as speaking up a little more easily, acting a little more assertively, or feeling a bit less self-critical. Recognize these as your suppressive system releasing glimmers of your core confidence. Persistently soak in reassurance and watch and wait for your suppressive system to release your confidence.

Enjoy Reassuring Your Way Out of Insecurity

Remember not to think of this as work. Instead, think of it as an adventure. Play with these exercises. The more you enjoy them, the more quickly you will recognize your suppressive thoughts until finally you will identify them as they're happening: "Oh, here I am covering up my confidence with doubt and self-criticism again."

When insecurity closes in on you, just put the Three-Step Action Plan into play. First, quickly see it as suppression. Second, welcome the instinctive anger that *moves* you to stop it. Third, enjoy channeling your energizing anger into soaking reassuring feelings into your suppressive system. Recognize suppression, get mad, and soak in reassurance! Recognize suppression, get mad, and soak in reassurance!

In the next chapter, you'll find visualizations carefully designed to reassure your suppressive system. Arrive prepared to play!

References

Denney, D. R., Sullivan, B. J., & Thiry, M. R. (1977). Participant modeling and self-verbalization training in the reduction of spider fears. *Journal of Behavior Therapy and Experimental Psychiatry, 8,* 247-53.

Denney, D. R., & Sullivan, B. J. (1976). Desensitization and modeling treatment of spider fears using two types of scenes. *Journal of Consulting and Clinical Psychology, 44,* 573-79.

Dillon, M., Minchoff, B., & Baker, K. (1985-86). Positive emotional states and enhancement of the immune system. *International Journal of Psychiatry in Medicine, 15,* 13-17.

Garfield, C. (1984). *Peak performance.* New York: Warner Books.

Gawain, S. (1978). *Creative visualization.* San Rafael, CA: Whatever Publishing.

Maltz, M. (1960). *Psycho-cybernetics.* New York: Prentice Hall.

Sullivan, B. J., & Denney, D. R. (1977). Expectancy and phobic level effects upon desensitization. *Journal of Consulting and Clinical Psychology, 45,* 763-71.

CHAPTER 7

Visualization Exercises

"To be a star and to stay a star, I think you've got to have a certain air of arrogance about you, a cockiness, a swagger on the field that says, 'I can do this and you can't stop me' . . . . I know that I play baseball with this air of arrogance, but I think it's lacking in a lot of guys who have the potential to be stars."
— JOE MORGAN, HALL OF FAME BASEBALL PLAYER

O ver the last 15 years I have repeatedly designed, tested, and redesigned these exercises into a simple technique easily absorbed by a primitive suppressive system.

I'm excited about presenting this program to you, but ultimately you will decide whether or not to pursue it. Take your time to absorb the program before you decide. Step back from pressuring yourself, also. It won't help. Being pushed makes part of your emotional system as rebellious as an angry adolescent.

Approach this program like a pleasant trip with an old friend. Remember the old Zen saying, "The journey is the reward."

These exercises won't make sense or be effective without the information provided earlier. You'll make progress much faster if you read the entire book first and review it frequently. Even the smartest clients don't absorb all that they need from their first reading. Your suppressive system absorbs information gradually, which is also why the exercises often restate messages.

In most cases, these exercises won't release bulletproof confidence in a day, a week, or even a month. Most people experience gradual, steady increases in confidence. For example, you may feel a bit bolder or a bit more assertive. Look for these gains and feel encouraged when you see them.

Moving ahead too quickly will very likely sensitize your suppressive system, causing it to overreact and deluge you with debilitating tension, confusion, and other negative feelings. Again, read the directions and warnings about moving too quickly in Chapter 6.

Anytime you feel stuck or have problems, reread Chapter 5 and Chapter 6.

To prepare for the first exercise, review the *What to Do When Insecurity Strikes* section in Chapter 6.

* * *

Exercise One: What to Do When Insecurity Strikes

We want this exercise to groove in an automatic response that will help you escape insecurity in those painful situations when it strikes. It's designed to create a vivid image or memory of insecurity striking you and train you to immediately initiate the steps to relieve it by recognizing it as suppression and channeling your anger into "soaking in" reassurance as discussed in Chapter 6.

If you have an accurate picture of your core confidence, you'll automatically see that your insecurities don't fit, and you'll recognize them as suppressive. Let's create that accurate image of yourself.

Remember your suppressive system responds much better to emotions, so in the following exercise and all later ones visualize your feelings as vividly as you can. Imagine yourself actually inside your body looking out through your eyes. If this is hard for you, begin by picturing yourself across the room.

Step One: Recognize Insecurities as Suppression

Recall a recent occasion when you began feeling your usual insecurities, self-doubts, or self-criticisms. You may have been about to confront someone, make a presentation, or join a group of strangers.

Imagine the scene as if it's happening right now. (It may help to close your eyes after reading each direction.)

Picture the scene and imagine feeling your usual suppressive anxiety or self-doubt surge into your mind and body.

Let this painful insecurity motivate you to say the following statements out loud.

- "This insecurity isn't my core nature."
- "This must be suppression hiding my core confidence."

Step Two: Let Your Healthy Anger Energize You

If you notice that this suppression irritates or angers you, say something out loud, for example, "I'm angry about this nagging insecurity." If you don't feel anger, you may be suppressing it with frustration or a sense of helplessness. In contrast, unsuppressed anger strengthens and energizes you to deal with problems. *Healthy anger will motivate you to soak lots of reassurance into your suppressive system.*

Imagine yourself feeling absolutely certain that you'll act sensibly while also allowing yourself to feel increasingly more intense levels of pure, energizing anger. Now express that healthy anger as you say out loud, "I'm going to soak reassurance into my suppressive system until it lets me believe in myself."

Step Three: Soaking In Reassuring Feelings

In the following visualization, you need to clearly feel that your strongest desire is to control all conceited or harmful actions. You need to surround your suppressive system with a gut-level sense that it's completely safe to feel your core confidence because you most want to act sensibly. We want to create images that will make your suppressive system take a deep breath, relax, and release your belief in yourself.

If you don't know how to feel that you're under control or how to feel that raw confidence is harmless, this may help: People often think that they're feeling when actually they're thinking about feeling. To help clarify the difference, imagine you're in a shopping mall with a bladder so full you want to step behind a potted plant and relieve yourself. You know that you won't. But you can also feel that you won't act on the urge. That's a feeling of control. It's a feeling of certainty. You need to feel certain that even if you feel cocky, your strongest desire will be to act sensibly.

It's important for you to decide for yourself in both your thinking and feeling brains that you can feel really good about yourself and still act sensibly!

Say the following statements out loud:

1. "I know from Core Confidence Theory that part of me feels that I'm terrific. But I also know that acting conceited will make people dislike and avoid me."
2. "I know that I want to avoid acting conceited. I can also feel that the biggest part of my emotional system wants to act sensibly."

The following statements invite even stronger feelings of control. These are your tools. Get to know and love them. Modify them if you like, but use them to invite sensuous, reassuring feelings into your body to calm your suppressive system.

These are not affirmations. We're not trying to persuade your emotional system that you're under control. We're inviting your emotional system to focus on and effortlessly exude a sense of certainty that you will safely contain your core confidence and act sensibly. Wait for the feeling to surface inside you, effortlessly.

The first time I present each statement, focus on the *feeling* of how much you want to act sensibly and how easily you can choose to act sensibly. When I present the statement a second time, let your *feeling* of certainty that you will act sensibly flow out as you say the statement out loud.

Focus on these words: I control what I say and do, so it's safe to feel good about myself.

Now say the words out loud: "I control what I say and do, so it's safe to feel good about myself."

Next, focus on these words: "I can feel really good about myself and keep that feeling safely inside my skin."

Now let the *feeling* roll out as you say the words, "I can feel really good about myself and contain that feeling safely inside my skin."

Wait for tiny flickers of this sense of certainty that you'll act sensibly. Waiting is important. Soaking in reassurance and then waiting opens the door for confidence. Pushing for a quick response slams it shut.

Because your core confidence is usually completely hidden, it's hard to imagine that you're constantly suppressing an inborn belief in your strength, worth, and talent under anxiety, self-doubt, and self-criticism. To uncover your core confidence, it's important to understand that it's there, that you don't have to build it, and that you simply need to get your suppressive system to relax and warm up to your deepest belief in yourself. Let's show your suppressive system that it's safe to enjoy *feeling really good about yourself* by visualizing that your strongest desire, what you most want, is to keep your life on the tracks by acting sensibly, no matter how good you feel about yourself.

In order for our ancestors to get to the top of the pecking order and survive, they needed an empowering belief that they should be at the top, that they were stronger, faster, smarter, better. They passed these intense empowering feelings to us. You can easily avoid acting on them, but feeling them is the only source of true confidence. The visualization below will show your suppressive system that you can safely feel them without acting on them. If you *worry* about acting cocky, uppity, or conceited, doesn't that mean you strongly *want* to avoid acting cocky or conceited and, instead, act sensibly— and that of course you will do so?

Avoid working at the following experience. After you put fertilizer on your lawn, you wait for your grass to absorb it. You don't have to do anything more. Show your suppressive system the following reassuring pictures and feelings and wait for it to absorb them, relax, and let your confidence surface. Simply wanting to discover your hidden confidence is enough. This desire automatically rivets your attention and mobilizes you.

The reassuring feeling stimulated by the following visualization is one of the most powerful active ingredients for relaxing your suppressive system. Make sure that you are feeling and not just thinking as you visualize. Your feelings influence your suppressive system the most.

* * *

My Favorite Self-Confidence Visualization

This exercise is my favorite because its images reassure your suppressive system the most powerfully. As you visualize, start with the highest of the following four levels of vividness that you can comfortably imagine.

- Level One: Visualize someone across the room as he feels and acts in that situation. (Visualizing someone else allows greater emotional distance from your feelings or less emotional involvement in them.)
- Level Two: Picture yourself across the room feeling and acting in the situation.
- Level Three: Imagine how another person feels as he looks out through his eyes at the scene.
- Level Four: Imagine yourself actually inside your body looking out through your eyes.

* * *

Part One: Reassuring Atmosphere

Close your eyes and imagine that your reason, wisdom, and common sense and your kindness, compassion, morals, and integrity are all symbolically present in the right side of your body.

Next to these, picture your wish to get along with people and your knowledge that acting conceited will make people dislike you.

Can you feel how much you value these parts of you? Can you feel how deeply committed you are to them and how determined you are to hold to them?

Imagine that what I call the "compassion and common sense action path" stretches out in front of these feelings. Picture yourself inside your mind looking out through your eyes and walking along this path, to the right. Imagine yourself acting warmly and considerately toward a few people on this path. Can you feel that your sensible, friendly, relationship-building actions such as being nice to people and respecting them will make them like you and admire you and smile when they see you. How much do you want their acceptance and admiration?

Do your compassion and common sense pull you toward these friendly actions? Images and feelings of how strongly you're drawn to act sensibly reassure your suppressive system that it's perfectly safe to imagine your survival instincts, specifically your inborn sense of worth and importance.

Keeping this feeling that your compassion and common sense firmly ground you on the right-hand path, can you feel that you want to discover your biological sense of worth and importance, your core feeling of I-feel-good-about-myself? Remember, this confidence made our ancestors feel that they deserved the warmest part of the cave. We should respect it as a legitimate survival strength, not fear or criticize it.

Imagine your inborn sense of worth on the left side of your body. (Some picture a peacock strutting, a stallion prancing, or a primate pounding its chest. Others recall a time when they felt really good about themselves, often as a young child, imagining they could do powerful things).

Feel how easy it is to completely contain your confidence inside your skin and still choose to act sensibly. This self-worth will make you feel strong and confident. Can you feel even brief glimpses of it?

If you begin to feel uncomfortable or uneasy, imagine your sensible feelings for a few moments. People often are uneasy. They're not used to feeling good about themselves. But core confidence is part of all of us. This exercise will help you feel safe and comfortable with your biological belief in yourself.

Imagine what I call "the arrogant action path" stretching out to the left in front of your core confidence. Picture yourself walking down this path acting cocky and swaggering toward a few people. Imagine their reactions.

Can you feel yourself automatically noting that these arrogant actions on the left-hand path might be five minutes of fun but would be followed by criticism and rejection?

Imagine yourself at a choice point between the two paths. Can you feel your emotional system automatically wanting the long-term benefits of acting sensibly because they're so much greater than the short-term pleasure of boasting, swaggering, or otherwise acting conceited?

Can you feel that your commitment to common sense and compassion and your determination to keep your life on the tracks make you want to choose the sensible right-hand action path?

Can you feel that this makes it perfectly, perfectly safe to imagine feeling an even deeper core sense of worth on your left side?

Wait for a stronger sense of your strength, talent, and importance to surface. This will include feelings such as "I'm capable, I'm attractive, and I feel really good about myself." These feelings will fill you with poise and confidence.

Can you feel that your cocky feelings excite and energize you to promote yourself, but that you still most want to act sensibly?

When you act sensibly, you still enjoy ninety percent of the short-term pleasure of feeling cocky, and you enjoy the long-term pleasure of people liking and admiring you.

Say: "I can feel raw confidence and prefer to act friendly."

Feeling your commitment and determination to keeping your life on the tracks by acting sensibly lets your suppressive system get a good, long look at how safe it is to uncover and feel more of your raw confidence.

Is it safe to look over your shoulder to the left at your cocky feelings and respect the strength, energy, and confidence they provide?

Even if you uncover your cockiest feeling, won't you still feel intellectually and emotionally committed to keeping your life on the tracks? Can you feel that you are determined to avoid cocky, offensive actions?

So is it safe to take these cocky feelings with you as you walk down your preferred right-hand path? With core confidence, you're fully functioning, standing tall, striding forward, and acting friendly. Your common sense and compassion help you form and enjoy good relationships, and your sense of worth and importance let you relax, smile, and enjoy radiating strength and poise. Experiencing all your feelings is a true win-win situation.

Like many pleasant daydreams, this one will roll along, entertaining you with deeper and more pleasurable inborn confidence. As it does, let the words, "This is perfectly safe, perfectly safe, perfectly safe, and harmless," effortlessly roll out of you.

Suppressive systems usually require repeated reassurance, and in the beginning, there often isn't any noticeable effect. Wait for them to work in the same way that you wait for fertilizer to strengthen your lawn. The more you show your suppressive system these pictures and feelings, the more it will relax and let you see more intense levels of your biological belief in your worth, strength, and talent.

Before beginning all reassuring visualizations, including those that I present later, visualize the above experience for a few minutes to create the all-important atmosphere of relaxed reassurance. This reassuring atmosphere is the most active ingredient for relaxing your suppressive system. Often, when visualizing situations in which you need more confidence, it helps to briefly move back to the reassuring images of your commitment to compassion and common sense and of you feeling drawn toward the right-hand path. Do this whenever a feeling of confidence isn't surfacing or has triggered nervousness, confusion, inadequacy, or any other suppressive feeling preventing or interrupting the flow of your confidence.

Part Two: Soaking In Reassurance in a Specific Setting

Keeping the above reassuring atmosphere intact, close your eyes and imagine that you're in a situation in which you need to feel more confident. Picture yourself inside your body looking out through your eyes at the situation.

Feel the nervousness, insecurity, or self-doubt that the situation stimulates.

Recognize this as suppression and say to yourself, "I need to reassure my suppressive system until it releases my inborn confidence."

Feel how strongly committed you are to acting friendly and unpretentious.

Do your thinking brain and your feeling brain both immediately recognize that acting on cocky, conceited feelings would be, at best, a short-term pleasure quickly followed by the long-term failure, rejection, and criticism that you know would come after acting conceited?

Can you clearly picture and feel in your body how costly acting conceited would be?

Are you strongly preferring and leaning toward the sensible right-hand, common sense-and-compassion path that creates the solid friendships and loving relationships that you want so much?

Is your feeling brain actively pulling you away from the arrogant and other aggressive actions along the exciting but destructive left-hand path? If it is, let that reassuring feeling sink all the way down into your suppressive system.

Can you clearly see and feel that choosing common sense and compassionate actions will make people feel good about you, want to be with you, and even admire you? Can you feel yourself pulling away from the obnoxious, self-centered path?

Can you feel that you want to avoid the rejection and criticism that come after a short-term pleasure of acting full of yourself?

Is your strongest desire to keep your life on the tracks, moving toward success, happiness, and good relationships by acting sensibly, not arrogantly? Hold this image in your mind and this feeling in your body so that your suppressive system can get a good, long look at how safe it is to feel really good about yourself.

As you lean toward the right-hand path, strongly preferring it, note how perfectly, perfectly safe it is to look back over your shoulder to the left-hand path and feel your strong, energizing, empowering belief in yourself. Because you're committed to acting sensibly, isn't it completely safe to feel really good about yourself?

Can you feel that you still prefer to do what makes people like you, admire you, and want to be with you? Are your desires to act sensibly creating an atmosphere of safety that makes you smile as your body relaxes and warms up to your core belief in yourself, that you're smart, cool, and strong? Note that this feeling is ninety-five percent of the pleasure. Actually acting on the feeling would add only an additional five percent and would bring along with it a slew of problems you don't want to experience.

Let this safe feeling become the atmosphere surrounding you. Let this pleasant visualization effortlessly roll on as a daydream that becomes stronger and deeper as your suppressive system continues to relax and let more sensuous levels of your belief in yourself surface.

Is it freeing and energizing to embrace your feelings that you're worthy and important?

Are you respecting and admiring the enlivening and empowering strength of your biological belief in yourself?

Say to yourself, "I can crimp my cockiness, or I can enjoy it and channel it into treating people well."

Part Three: Combining the Steps

Let's replay the visualization of an insecurity-inducing situation from the previous exercise so you can respond with all three steps: recognize suppression, get mad, and soak in reassurance.

Look out through your eyes at the other people in the scene and feel in your body your usual suppressive anxiety or self-criticism surge over you. You may be feeling silly, stupid, or unattractive. You may be telling yourself, "I'm not good enough," or "I can't do it." Your stomach may be tense, your mouth dry, or your palms clammy.

Recognize this as suppression. Notice that insecurity doesn't fit with your core confidence.

Say out loud, "I shouldn't be insecure. I should be feeling capable. My confidence must be too hot for my suppressive system."

Recognize that your suppressive system is stealing your inborn belief in yourself. Say something like, "This makes me mad; I need to believe in myself." Can you feel this anger make you want to stop the suppression?

Don't push to feel angry. Focus on the words, "This insecurity makes me mad, but I'm going to act sensibly and wait for irritation or anger to come up naturally."

Now let your anger roll out as you say aloud, "I'm going to keep soaking in reassurance."

You already know that it wouldn't be good to act conceited. Just focus on that comfortable feeling of certainty that you'll act sensibly so your suppressive system can relax. To make that feeling stronger, imagine feeling drawn toward the common sense-and-compassion path from the earlier exercise.

Invite deeper feelings of control by using a reassuring statement. If you don't have a favorite yet, focus on this one: "I control what I say and do, so it's safe to feel good about myself."

Now say out loud, "I control what I say and do, so it's safe to feel good about myself."

Ask yourself: what hidden confidence would likely be stimulated by this situation and might be triggering your suppression? Do you secretly want to swagger into a group? Do you feel you're the coolest one there? Ask yourself, "What kind of raw confidence would this situation normally cause?"

Now zero in on that particular confident feeling. Notice that you're not moving to actually do it. You're not going to swagger or act in any way offensive.

See yourself acting normally and soak in your strongest feeling of wanting to act sensibly.

So it's safe to feel really good about yourself. It's even safe to feel wildly confident. Feel yourself easily keeping your actions appropriate.

Statements that invite you to feel physically certain of your control will reassure your suppressive system the fastest and bring more confidence. Compose your own if you wish! Keep them handy, and say them whenever insecurity strikes. Soon you'll recognize your suppression as it's happening.

Remember, you've got to blindly soak reassurance into your suppressive system, and you have to soak it in again and again—usually without any noticeable effect. It takes time for the reassurance to sink in. Sometimes in important situations, such as presentations or job interviews, it may seem there is nothing inside you but fear and weakness. You may feel that you're the one person born without core confidence. If you don't continue to blindly soak in reassurance, you may never move beyond insecurity.

If you do persist, your suppressive system will gradually allow your core confidence to rise inside you. Say out loud, "I need more reassurance because I want to believe in myself."

> *Look for small increases in confidence, such as speaking up a little more easily, acting a little more assertively, or feeling a bit less self-critical. These improvements mean your suppressive system is releasing a bit more of your core confidence. Tell yourself, "Good job!"*
>
> When insecurities strike, uncovering your belief in yourself is the most important game in town, and you're going to win it because you're that good! You're that persistent, and you want confidence that bad!

Four Additional Visualization Exercises

Again, begin all visualization exercises by creating an atmosphere of reassurance. Picture your compassion, friendliness, and common sense on the right side of your body and visualize these pulling you down the right-hand, common sense-and-compassion action path. This is the most active ingredient in the program.

Each additional visualization is followed by a brief version called a Quick Phrase Confidence Releaser to use when time is limited.

The I Feel Good About Myself Visualization

Before doing this exercise, briefly review Chapter 5. Imagine you're with people you respect, and you want to feel more confident. You may be making a presentation or in a social or business gathering.

Because you want these people to like and respect you, you want to act friendly and sensibly, no matter how good you feel about yourself. You want to avoid swaggering, boasting, or other offensive, conceited actions. You must decide for yourself in both your thinking and feeling brain that you will choose to act sensibly.

Notice how easily you can act appropriately no matter what you feel. Now focus on the words, "I feel good about myself." Wait for the feeling to come up naturally, like hunger comes.

Now say out loud, "I feel good about myself." If you can feel even slightly good about yourself, let it build for a moment and note how harmless it is. You may not notice the feeling yet, so to let your suppressive system warm up to it, again, focus on the words, "I feel good about myself" and wait for the feeling.

Now let that feeling come out as you say aloud, "I feel good about myself."

Are you *thinking* that you feel good about yourself or are you really experiencing the *feeling* in your body? Many people think the feel good about themselves, but fail to recognize that they're not feeling much at all. We need to uncover your sensuous physical experience.

Once more, feeling certain that you will act sensibly, focus on the words, "I feel good about myself," and let the emotion surface. Now say out loud, "I feel good about myself."

Were you pushing or hurrying or coaxing yourself? Remember, coaxing is not the same thing as waiting for your suppressive system to relax and release your inborn belief in yourself. If you're coaxing yourself, relax, breathe deep, and let go.

Picture yourself feeling good about yourself and still greeting people with a warm, "Good morning, how are you?" Could you imagine feeling double that confidence and still acting friendly?

Soak in these reassuring images and wait confidently; sooner or later your suppressive system will let that first tiny good feeling about yourself effortlessly rise inside you. Even if, at first, it's only the faintest glimmer of self-worth, your suppressive system will gradually warm up to it.

You know what's smart to do, and you know what's not smart to do. And only the smart, *thinking* part of your brain can control your actions, because it's in the same part of your brain as your movement centers, and it's well connected to them. Your feeling centers are in a different part of your brain and aren't well connected to your movement centers, so feeling valuable can't ever *make* you actually strut through the office.

Feeling certain that you can act sensibly, focus on the words, "I feel good about myself." Let a glimmer of self-worth roll out naturally as you say the words, "I feel good about myself."

If you feel bored, silly, or otherwise distracted, that's probably your suppressive system. You won't be able to see or feel your suppressive system getting alarmed and flooding your mind with these distractions. Negative feelings just appear. Let your suppressive system relax as you not just think but feel how much your compassion, conscience, and common sense make you want to control your core confidence.

If you really felt that you were smarter, more talented, or better looking than others, would you prance around demanding that they admire you? Of course not! You might love feeling smarter and more talented, but you really don't want to be seen as a conceited jerk. Right now, say out loud, "It's fun to *feel* really good about myself, but I'm going to *act* friendly."

The longer your suppressive system watches you feeling good about yourself while acting sensibly, the more it relaxes and the more of your confidence it releases. Take on a confident posture. Stick out your chest. Focus on the words, "I feel really good about myself." Let the feeling come up naturally.

Now let the feeling roll out as you say, "I feel really good about myself."

Did you feel a glimmer of healthy self-worth? If this feeling were twice as strong, could you still decide to act normally?

Even if you don't feel much yet, say the words to let your suppressive system warm up to them.

Once more, take a deep breath and stick out your chest. Smile and focus on the words, "I feel really good about myself," and wait for the feeling to come. Now let it roll out as you say aloud, "I feel really good about myself."

You know this confidence is harmless, but your suppressive system has to feel that it's harmless. So stick out your chest once more, smile, and focus on the words, "I feel really good about myself." Wait for the feeling. Now say, "I feel really good about myself."

Did you feel even slightly more self-worth? All you need is a gradual increase in confidence. Soon you could enjoy empowering confidence most of the time.

Quick Phrase Confidence Releaser

During the day when you don't have time for the complete exercise above, imagine yourself in a situation in which you need to feel confident. Focus on the words, "It's perfectly safe for me to feel really good about myself." Wait for the feelings to come, and then express them out loud. Then enjoy imagining feeling really good about yourself and still acting friendly and sensibly.

The Welcoming Instinctive Worthiness Visualization

Before doing this exercise, briefly review Chapter 6, especially the sections on troubleshooting and visualizing from inside your body. It's important for you to decide at both a thinking and a feeling level that you can feel worthy and still act sensibly.

Feeling good about yourself and still acting sensibly is as easy as feeling hurried but choosing not to run a red light. Your thinking brain is in the driver's seat holding the steering wheel, and your feeling brain is in the trunk impulsively yelling, "Hurry up!" The smart, reasonable parts of your brain will make you stop at a red light. If no one were around, you might decide to run the light. But if there's a semi coming at you, your smart brain systems are going to keep your foot on the brake no matter how loudly your feeling systems are yelling. Your feeling systems can't make you do anything. No matter how valuable you feel, you're thinking brain will still remember that acting conceited costs too much.

Imagine a situation in which you want more confidence, such as standing up for yourself, introducing yourself at a party, or interviewing for a job or promotion.

Adjust the scene and the people to your needs and liking.

Look out through your eyes at the other people and feel in your body how much you want them to like and respect you.

Feel how easily you can decide to be friendly and charming. You compliment the other people and ask them to talk about themselves. You smile, feeling really good about yourself, yet you still want to say nice things to them. You appear enthusiastic, confident, and charming.

If you feel really good about yourself, will the others be less happy? No.

Say out loud, "It's perfectly safe for me to feel valuable and worthy."

Don't push or try. Just soak in this reassurance and wait for your suppressive system to relax and release your confidence. Now say out loud, "It's perfectly safe for me to feel valuable and worthy."

Core confidence was stamped into your body at birth by evolution. It can't be absent. Feeling confident should be easy. Once more, focus on the words, "It's perfectly safe for me to feel valuable and worthy," and wait for the feeling to surface. Now say out loud, "It's perfectly safe for me to feel valuable and worthy."

As you look at the people in the scene, remember that your ancestors needed to automatically feel at least equal to their peers or they would have been pushed to the bottom of the pecking order. You, too, were born feeling at least as worthy as everyone around you. If you don't feel this inborn worthiness, your suppressive system is paralyzing it.

As you look at the other people, invite your body to generate the instinctive good feelings about yourself that will gain you respect and acceptance in the group.

You can believe in yourself, and your compassion and thinking systems will still work. They will make you feel friendly and want to act nicely. You can feel worthy and also want to act toward others with compassion. Do you decide to control other strong feelings, such as the attractions you feel toward good-looking strangers in the mall? And you always decide not to grab their fannies, don't you?

Again, picture the scene and focus on the words, "I can feel worthy and still care about others."

Let the feeling surface as you say out loud, "I can feel worthy and still care about others."

Look at the other people in the scene and take a confident posture. Sit taller and stick out your chest. Feel how much you want to act friendly and appropriate. Feel certain that you will act sensibly. Focus on the words, "Deep inside, I feel worthy." Now let that feeling roll out as you say out loud, "Deep inside, I feel worthy."

Focus on the words, "I was born to be at the top of the pecking order," and let the feeling come up effortlessly.

Now let the feeling roll out of you as you say out loud, "I was born to be at the top of the pecking order." Now say, "I will act nicely, but feeling worthy was stamped into my body at birth."

Feel the sensual pleasure of this confident worthiness inside your body!

You may have to start with less than a flicker of worthiness. Each time you do these exercises, let your suppressive system get a good long look at your sense of worthiness and warm up to it.

Once you've felt worthy, whenever you don't feel it, say, "I need more reassurance because I want that worthy feeling back!"

Quick Phrase Confidence Releaser

When you don't have time for the complete exercise above, imagine yourself in a situation in which you need to feel confident, and say, "It's perfectly safe for me to feel that I was born to feel worthy," and wait for the feelings. Remember, this is a feeling. It doesn't have to be a fact.

Right now, try on the power of your confidence. Again, imagine yourself in the scene and let your suppressive system watch you safely enjoying the pleasure and passion of feeling really good about yourself. Focus on the words, "I was born to feel worthy," and wait for the feeling.

Now let that feeling rollout effortlessly, as you say out loud, "I was born to feel worthy." Now continue seeing and feeling your deep sense of worthiness influencing the others and drawing them to you and your ideas and goals.

The I Am Smart and Talented Visualization

Close your eyes and imagine yourself in a new situation in which you feel insecure. You may be confronting someone, asking for a raise, preparing to perform, or trying to make conversation. Feel yourself actually in the scene looking out through your eyes.

Maybe you feel unattractive or not good enough. Anxiety or self-doubt may surge through your body. Recognize your insecurity as suppression.

Say out loud, "I can't see why my suppressive system is doing this, but I know this insecurity is probably paralyzing the raw confidence I need."

Now say something like, "This makes me mad; I need to believe in myself." Let your anger mobilize you to stop the suppression.

Ask yourself, "What kind of specific core confidence is triggering this suppression?" Possibly you're unconsciously feeling a sense of importance, that you're the big cheese.

Now let your anger energize you to make the following reassuring statements out loud. "Even if I feel good about myself from the top of my head to the tip of my toes, I'm going to act sensibly." Wait for the feeling to surface.

Now say, "Even if I feel smarter or more talented than others, I'm going to smile and act friendly."

Now say, "I can feel like the big cheese, and still act sensibly."

Feeling worthy is fun, but it's still only a feeling, safely enclosed inside your skin. It can't get out and hurt anyone. Does anyone else even know that you feel it? No, of course not! If you walked into a group feeling great about yourself, would anyone even know that? Why not just enjoy *feeling*, "I'm terrific," and decide to *act* normally?

Picture yourself looking out at the other people in the scene again and feel certain that you'll act sensibly. Feel how much you don't want to look snooty or stuck-up. No, you don't want that! Feel yourself preferring to act sensibly.

Also feel that you'll do much better with people if you speak and act from your kind and friendly feelings.

Would you actually swagger and proclaim, "I am the big cheese?" Of course not! You must decide for yourself. Is it perfectly safe for you to feel, "I'm the most talented," if you completely contain it inside your skin?

Feel yourself wanting to act sensibly and choosing to act sensibly.

Even if you aren't the smartest or most desirable person, feeling that you are will still help you perform at your absolute best, completely focused on winning, the way you were meant to.

Michael Jordan's feeling, "Whenever we need it, I always believe I can do it," wasn't a fact, but it helped him perform magnificently. Bird strikes knocked out the jet engines of heroic US Airways pilot Chesley B. Sullenberger III's AirBus 80 with 155 passengers and forced him to masterfully land in New York's Hudson River. He'd never before crash-landed a plane, but in a post-crash *60 Minutes* interview, he radiated complete confidence when he said, "I knew I could do it."

This is not a time for thinking or judging whether or not you are actually the smartest or most talented. This is a time for feeling smart, talented, and worthy.

Relax and again look at the people in the scene as you focus on the words, "I'm smart, talented, and worthy." Stick out your chest and wait for the feelings.

Now say out loud, "I'm smart, talented, and worthy!"

Believing in yourself feels really good, and you want to contain it, because you want people to like and respect you.

When talking with an attractive, sexy person, you enjoy feeling sexual and still decide to act appropriately, don't you? Could you also enjoy feeling that you're smart, talented, and worthy and decide to act friendly and sensibly?

Five gallons of boiling water could burn someone badly. But diluted in a swimming pool of cool water, it's harmless. Similarly, five gallons of boiling belief in yourself in a swimming pool of compassion and common sense is harmless. Imagine a feeling that you are the most worthy boiling up in your body right now but completely surrounded by a pool full of compassion and common sense.

Don't try to make yourself believe these words. Just let words come to mind that will open the door for your healthy confidence to surge up and fill you with an energizing belief in yourself.

Look at the people in the scene and focus on the words, "I'm smart and talented," and you're really going to think, "I'm terrific." Wait for the feeling.

Now let it roll out as you say out loud, "I'm smart and talented, and you're really going to think I'm terrific!"

If you didn't say those words out loud, would anyone even know that you felt that?

Visualize feeling this confidence and enjoy the fact that it's your secret.

Once more, look out through your eyes and see the other people in the scene.

Focus on the words, "I'm smart and talented, and you're really going to think I'm terrific," and wait for the feeling.

Now let the feeling roll out as you say these words or something like them, "I'm smart and talented, and you're really going to think I'm terrific!"

Are you still able to act sensibly? Did anything burst into flame?

Once more focus on the words, "I'm smart and talented, and you're really going to think I'm terrific!"

Now say out loud, "I'm smart and talented, and you're really going to think I'm terrific!"

See your delightful confidence fueling an alluring, radiant sense of being alive?

Let your suppressive system watch as you naturally channel this confidence into a rolling daydream of success. Every day, take time to let your daydreams wander through more and more pleasurable vignettes of you as smart, talented, and worthy. Each one will relax your suppressive system more.

Quick Phrase Confidence Releaser

When you only have a few moments, imagine a situation in which you want more confidence. As before, focus on a statement such as, "It's perfectly safe for me to feel smart, talented, and worthy." Wait for the feeling, and then let it roll out as you say out loud, "It's perfectly safe for me to feel, smart, talented, and worthy."

Now soak in that reassuring feeling that it's perfectly safe to feel smart, talented, and worthy.

Now focus on the words, "I can safely feel like the big dog because I most want to act sensibly!"

Now let your confident feeling roll out as you say out loud, "It's perfectly safe to feel like the big dog because that clears my mind and makes me friendlier."

Now say, "I'm the big dog."

The I Am Magic, I Can Do Anything Visualization

Before doing this exercise, briefly review Chapter 5. Strong sexual instincts caused our prehistoric ancestors to procreate and survive. Those of us with compassion and conscience feel strong sexual desires and act sensibly about them. Similarly, our ancestors also survived because an instinctive sense of importance and superiority made them feel entitled to eat first and sleep closest to the fire. Though we can easily choose to act friendly and unpretentiously about these feelings of importance, most of us fear and usually deny them because we don't want to become pompous. Yet these feelings were put into our bodies by evolution, and they are inescapable. They won't go away because we don't like them or don't want them.

If you try this exercise before you're ready to feel your instinctive sense of importance, your suppressive system may shutdown so hard that it permanently hides the confidence you want. Stop if you feel anxious or uneasy and continue with previous exercises until you're more comfortable.

Feeling important and superior isn't optional—it's standard equipment in human bodies. Uncovering your sense of importance lets it join your conscience, compassion, generosity, and other caring emotions. It doesn't erase or lessen them.

You can walk, talk, and think all at the same time because different brain systems generate each behavior. One brain system can be repulsed by someone's bad breath and other brain systems can decide not to mention it. Similarly, core confidence systems do make you feel superior, and yet, other systems *will make you care about people and act sensibly* all at the same time.

Feeling superior won't make you delusional. Your thinking mind won't go on vacation. It knows that you can't *do everything*, that you aren't magic, and that you won't always win or get the job. But these facts can hurt your performance. Set them on a shelf inside you so that they don't smother the boiling belief in yourself that can fill you with the sense of worthiness you need *to confront someone, stand up for yourself, tell good jokes and stories, or let criticism and rejection bounce off you.* You perform at your best when you feel that you're magic, that you can do anything.

We're going to find the buried feeling place inside you that does believe that you're so good that you're magic, that you can get any job, make any speech, sell any customer, and attract any partner.

Then we're going to get your suppressive system to release more and more of these feelings until they fill you with the sensual experience that you're magic, that you can do anything.

Imagine yourself inside your body looking out through your eyes at a group of people. Imagine caring about them but also feeling a deep belief in yourself.

Say out loud, "I care about these people and want them to like me."

Though you want something in a store, you feel certain that you won't steal it. Similarly, feel certain that you can release your strongest belief in yourself and still act sensibly.

Remember, this is not a time for facts; this is a time to find and feel empowered by your inborn feeling: "I'm terrific; I can do anything." Stick out your chest and focus on the words, "I'm terrific; I can do anything," and wait for the feeling.

Now let it effortlessly roll out as you say, "I'm terrific; I can do anything."

Let this feeling surface and enjoy its physical form. Stick out your chest, hold your head high, and invite the cocky feeling.

Now say, "I'm terrific; I can do anything."

Isn't this a great feeling? Isn't this harmless?

Now imagine yourself in an important situation, such as meeting new people or standing up for yourself.

Feel how easily you can act appropriately even if you feel that you're wonderful.

Right now, focusing on this sense of control in your body, say out loud, "I can feel that I'm magic and still act friendly."

Once more, focus on the words, "I am magic, I can do anything," and wait for the raw confidence to come up as naturally as you salivate when a waiter brings out a sizzling dinner.

Now let the feeling roll out as you say, "I am magic, I can do anything!"

If you didn't say the words publicly, would anyone even know how you felt? Is it perfectly safe to enjoy feeling that you're magic? Would this innate self-worth make you look good, feel poised, and perform at your best? Once more, look out through your eyes and see the other people in the scene.

Raise your head and stick out your chest as you focus on the words, "I am a force of nature! Nothing can stand in my way!"

Now let your core confidence roll out as you say out loud, "I am a force of nature! Nothing can stand in my way!"

See yourself as the smartest, strongest, and most capable.

Now relax and let even more feeling roll out as you say out loud, "I am a force of nature! Nothing can stand in my way!"

Did this confidence create any problems at all? Is it perfectly safe to feel, "I am a force of nature?" Sure it is!

Don't work or push. Invite this confidence to come forward. Play with it. Walk or sit with your head high and your chest out. Enjoy swaggering. Wait for this instinctive belief in yourself, and when it comes, let it roll out into some words or appropriate actions. *It's fun to feel that you're magic!*

It should always feel wonderful. If it feels dull or repetitive, your suppressive system is at work. Once you've felt flickers of that "I am magic" feeling, whenever you don't feel it, say, "I need more reassurance because I want that magic feeling back."

Frequently during each day open your mind to rolling daydreams. Imagine yourself in various situations in which you want more confidence, and say, "It's perfectly safe for me to feel that I am magic." Then wait for the feelings.

Let your daydreams wander pleasurably onward through scene after scene to an ever deepening sense of being terrific. You were born to feel that you're magic.

Don't fight suppressive anxiety and insecurity. Let your biological strength, your belief in yourself, come on up. Rock and roll!

Creating Visualizations for Specific Situations

The following are two examples of situations in which peoples' suppressive systems commonly choke off the instinctive survival strengths that the settings stimulate. You can relieve your anxieties in these and many different situations by plugging the specific scenarios into the exercises you've learned.

Assertiveness Setting

People report most frequently wanting more confidence in confronting someone, standing up for themselves, and saying no. Many people criticize themselves as too cowardly to be assertive in these situations, but as you know by now, this self-criticism is a suppressive veneer covering the unconscious competitive drive instinctively stimulated by the pressure of these settings, which usually sets in motion a primordial desire for the alpha position in the social hierarchy.

Remember that your ancestors survived because intense automatic feelings fueled them to push hard to win these types of competitions. As a result, when competitive situations arise, whether or not you are aware of your primordial instincts and whether or not you approve of them, your core confidence systems will reflexively generate feelings that you are superior and entitled to dominance. "I am right; you should do what I want," and "I am more important and can say no to you," are examples of such feelings.

Many of my clients' suppressive systems are so hypersensitive to feeling superior that they generate intense anxiety and self-criticism to completely bury any sense of superiority whenever they are in pressure situations. Sometimes they can't even bear hearing me talk about feeling superior. As a result, they have a hard time understanding that they are unconsciously feeling so superior that their suppressive systems are paralyzing them with anxiety, hesitancy, or self-criticism.

If you want to feel so confident that you can confront others, say no, or stand up for yourself, you will have to get your suppressive system to warm up to those aggressive strengths that were put into your body to help you survive.

For example, when you confront someone, you are taking the more powerful position of calling him or his behavior into question. You are trying to change him. No matter how nicely someone asks you to do something, they are symbolically pushing you. When you say no, you have pushed back.

Add this assertiveness setting to any of the previous exercises. For example, imagine yourself confronting someone, standing up for yourself, or saying no to someone. Begin visualizing very mild levels of confidence and gradually increase these feelings as you feel more comfortable. If you want to feel really confident (meaning completely free of suppressive insecurity), you're going to have to accept the *spine-tingling* sense of superiority and entitlement that are standard equipment in human bodies. If you feel these emotions, you can act on them. However, your strongest desires to act sensibly will make it easy to choose to act compassionately and unpretentiously.

The type of person who would read this book usually most wants to act unpretentiously. Remember that you most want to act sensible, not superior. Do this at both a thinking and feeling level.

Feel Confident Making Presentations and Telling Jokes and Stories

About eighty-five percent of people fear public speaking. They worry about making mistakes or not being good enough. They feel anxious about embarrassing themselves.

Successful actors, singers, speakers, storytellers, entertainers, and other performers are usually able to feel core confidence at least while they're performing. Many of them may have suppressive systems that generate insecurities in other situations. Michael Caine's statement, "All actors have big egos," suggests that feeling really good about yourself is important in performing in front of people. If you're having difficulty feeling confident in any of these speaking, performing, or entertaining arenas, recognize that being in front of an audience naturally stimulates our emotional systems to generate the same feelings of superiority that would have energized our ancestors to gain the most power, influence, and dominance. These unavoidable instinctive reflexes include intense emotions you may consider unappealing, such as "I am wonderful!" Even if you consider this raw confidence appalling, the more you persuade your suppressive system that you can safely enjoy and control deeper levels of it, the less it will inject you with anxiety and insecurity whenever you're in front of an audience.

References

Ferguson, H. (1983). *The edge.* Cleveland: Getting the Edge Company.
Sullenberger III, C. (2009). *60 minutes* [Television Broadcast January 15] New York: CBS.

CHAPTER 8

Meet Your Drill Sergeant

"Modesty is the lowest of the virtues, and is a real confession of the deficiency it indicates. One who undervalues himself is justly undervalued by others."
—WILLIAM HAZLITT

When people perform (or prepare to perform) for work, school, or social activities, they may feel tense or insecure. They may misperceive that anxiety or nervousness arises from poor self-confidence. Suppressive insecurities can make your mouth dry, your palms sweat, or your stomach knot up. But for many people, even after they are comfortable with and stop suppressing core confidence, similar tense feelings remain. Kate Nelson uncovered strong core confidence and felt better during sales presentations, but she still felt distressing tension. We looked closely at this tension and found that it had nothing to do with suppressive self-criticisms or feelings of inadequacies and everything to do with her demand that she accomplish more than was humanly possible. This demand was generated by an inborn, emotional brain system that drives us to fix problems, accomplish goals, and strive to be smarter, stronger, and faster. I call it a "Drill Sergeant Self-Driving" system.

It could be argued that your self-driving drill sergeant is an extremely intense level of normal desire. It is easier and, I suspect, more accurate to conceptualize it as a desire generated by a separate brain system that is like an overpowered turbo booster, stripping the gears and eventually burning out the engine.

These unrelenting demands paralyze your healthy motivational system that can make you excited and eager to accomplish goals. For example, if you wanted to become an artist, your healthy motivational system might make you feel eager to take art classes or read books on painting. This motivation system generates an energizing feeling of wanting, not a debilitating, exhausting feeling of pushing and insisting. It's powerful and effective, yet much less consuming. It makes you feel good. It spawns flexibility, ingenuity, and creativity. Your drill sergeant pounds you into a narrow, rigid mindset, creating frustration, exhaustion, hopelessness, and self-doubt.

Kate mistook her tension for a confidence problem because her drill sergeant drove her to feel she hadn't done enough or should do more, better, faster. It shamed, humiliated, and criticized her, but the resulting bad feelings were different than and separate from her suppressive insecurities and self-criticisms.

You too may have a secret drill sergeant that pushes you toward perfection. Your drill sergeant may make you regret your mistakes or feel guilty when you take time for pleasure. Life is not all about work, and the drill sergeant stands in the way of your contentment. It prevents you from letting go of impossible goals that you know you should abandon. It makes you indecisive, forcing you to analyze the pros and cons of even minor choices again and again, insisting on absolute certainty about what is best. These criticisms and self-doubt aren't fabricated to suppress confidence and can't be relieved by uncovering more confidence. You may mistake the tension from this distressing pressure as suppressive insecurity and may not recognize that your drill sergeant is driving you mercilessly. You may miss an opportunity to get it to stop.

I believe that the drill sergeant once had an important place in the lives of humans. Evolution created your drill sergeant and its relentless demand for more success and improvement to help you survive. In primitive times, inner drill sergeants helped our ancestors survive, driving them, for example, to pursue game for days. Without this intense motivation, humankind might have given up and starved to death. Unfortunately, your self-driving system is so constraining and narrowly focused that it helps you succeed only in very straightforward behavioral tasks, such as searching for water or pursuing a fleeing wounded caribou.

Your daily activities, such as thinking, planning, and calculating are much more complex than pursuing game. Self-driving is rarely, if ever, helpful in complex activities, and in most situations, it's downright debilitating—the equivalent of whacking yourself with a ruler to make you think faster.

Unfortunately, no matter how much work you get done, there is always more, and so your drill sergeant demands more and more. Life becomes a rat race, with endless lists of worrisome tasks. You never seem to have enough time to enjoy life, family, and friends. A friend of mine once described his feeling of being rushed through life in terms of someone pouring gas on his fanny every morning and lighting it. While we don't all feel that rushed, our drill sergeant makes the majority of us suffer every day, ordering us to be faster, smarter, or stronger.

One reason you don't consciously recognize your drill sergeant pushing you is that its demands usually trigger your suppressive system to control and cover its aggressiveness by generating additional paralyzing anxiety, depression, self-doubt, or inadequacy, which you may incorrectly attribute to insufficient confidence. For example, one of my clients cleaned his clothes and his car obsessively before he dated girlfriends. He thought he did so because he lacked confidence in his attractiveness. We discovered that actually his confidence was high, but his drill sergeant demanded, "You must be perfect enough to make women swoon." This intense demand alarmed his suppressive system, which instantly generated feelings of inadequacy to camouflage it.

People who feel anxious making presentations often conclude that they need more confidence. For decades, whenever I spoke in public, my palms were so wet that I was embarrassed to shake hands, and my armpits soaked through my shirt and suit coat. My drill sergeant drove me to spend a hundred hours perfecting a one-hour speech. I thought that I was just nervous and needed more confidence. Although my suppressive feelings of inadequacy had generated some of my tension, the tension wasn't fully eliminated even after I uncovered strong core confidence.

When I looked carefully at these remaining tense feelings to discover why my improved self-confidence hadn't relieved them, I noticed that they felt different than suppressive inadequacies. My drill sergeant was demanding, "This speech isn't fluent or witty; you need to *mesmerize!*" It was determined to drive me ceaselessly until I spoke as eloquently as John F. Kennedy, as passionately as Dr. Martin Luther King, Jr., and as humorously as Robin Williams. (I was zero for three.)

My drill sergeant was so intense and its expectations so unreasonable that I first called it a Fanatical Insistence System. Many clients didn't like to think of themselves as having an internal fanatic, so I renamed it a Drill Sergeant Self-Driving system. Yet, for many, this drill sergeant is so severe and irrational that it feels fanatical.

A 40-year-old male client described his drill sergeant driving him to climb to the summit of the second tallest mountain in the world. He said, "It was thirty below zero, and I had only climbed one other mountain. There were twenty-three of us, and most of the others, including a personal trainer and an ex-pro football player, were in much better shape than me. Yet only two of us made it to the summit. My drill sergeant pounded me all the way to the top, 'Don't you dare quit, you wimp. Keep putting one foot in front of the other, one foot in front of the other—do it!'"

Though he succeeded, his healthy desire to climb the mountain and to enjoy doing it would have motivated him less harshly and more effectively without draining his energies. The experience would certainly have been more satisfying. He realized that his drill sergeant drove him many times every day. He also realized that in problem-solving or when engaged in anything more than simple routine behaviors like putting one foot in front of the other, such intense pressure is debilitating. It's like struggling to think or plan with someone screaming in your ear.

There's another reason why we tend not to recognize our drill sergeant. Drill sergeants generate vague, nonverbal feelings, often without any thoughts attached. Because feelings arise in the emotional part of the brain that isn't well connected to the intelligent part, it's as if your drill sergeant is working undercover, making you feel harried, frustrated, and exhausted as you struggle to meet deadlines, achieve your dreams, or be "good enough." You don't consciously recognize the harsh, relentless, unforgiving part of your emotional system generating a nonverbal feeling of urgency that pressures you like a recruit in boot camp, insisting that you never be late, always make the best choice, or never say the wrong thing.

You probably believe that your bad feelings are caused by your poor confidence or the people and problems in your life. For example, one of my clients felt that raising her three children caused her enormous stress. Raising children is stressful, but her secret drill sergeant caused the majority of her stress by demanding that she parent perfectly, vehemently refusing to accept the unavoidable failures that all parents have. Often you can't identify why you worry or obsess, and you wonder why you can't just let things go. The reason your unintelligent, pushy brain system keeps demanding that you succeed, resolve the situation, or even save the world is because it isn't smart enough to understand that many things are impossible or not sensible to do. For example, people who struggle with indecision often conclude that they don't have enough self-confidence to trust their decisions. But in many situations they simply don't have enough facts to clearly identify which is the best choice. Instead of logically deciding as best they can and moving on, their pushy brain system demands that they keep analyzing and re-analyzing.

The logical thinking parts of your brain know that you can't close every sale, please every boss, or solve every problem—and they know you don't have to. Yet your drill sergeant can't understand this. It wants total victory at all times, and it feels that if it keeps pounding you with deeper guilt, greater urgency, higher standards, or meaner criticism, it will eventually force you to perform flawlessly. It will push you to do whatever it takes to succeed, and it won't understand that it will exhaust and eventually kill you. Nor would it care if it did.

Our drill sergeant is often so aggressive that we don't want to believe that any part of us could feel so mean. For example, a client of mine, a successful business executive, hid his self-driving feelings by perceiving that his boss created his stress and nervousness. I described the harsh feelings hiding under his work stress this way: "Your feeling toward yourself is, 'I want to hurt you until you perform so well that your boss can never criticize you.' Emotionally, you want to slam your head into a door jamb until you're that good."

He said, "That's awful! Who would want to be like that? If any part of me is like that . . . oh, no, no, I can't possibly have those feelings." Later he was able to intellectually understand that these self-driving feelings were part of his biology. However, it took several more sessions before he was able to actually stop suppressing and then clearly experience his harsh feelings. Once he did, it was easy for him to decide not to slam his head into a door jamb.

Helping Your Drill Sergeant Learn to Stop and Let Go

To escape this harsh master, you must look beneath your stress, anxiety, and frustration to sense your drill sergeant at work. Then you must teach it to recognize that its relentless, primitive push to succeed brings you only misery and feelings of failure. It needs to become self-aware and recognize that it creates that terrible sensation of not measuring up, of failure. It has to experience this so often that it finally responds to it with, "No, I'm not stepping into that negative arena because I'll just make myself endlessly miserable. I can't fix this problem or right this injustice. If I keep pressuring myself, I will ruin every day of my life."

Unfortunately, as I've mentioned, your drill sergeant hangs out in the unintelligent, emotional part of your brain. It's probably unaware of itself and of its destructiveness. Even when your logical thinking brain says, "Let go of this; I can't make this perfect," the drill sergeant doesn't understand, and it doesn't stop pushing. It has one simple purpose: to generate an overwhelming feeling that you must struggle harder and harder to reach your goal. It automatically makes you feel that if you haven't succeeded, you should work harder.

Your self-driving system can, however, "learn" from mental pictures and feelings that you show it—pictures and feelings of its exhausting persistence that bring failure and misery. Frequently imagining or experiencing these pictures and feelings can teach it to let go and stop its debilitating demands. These visualizations are most effective if they are vivid and sensory, so that your drill sergeant can physically experience and connect its intense demanding to the exhaustion, anxiety, and failure that it produces.

Most of us have great difficulty grasping how to even begin this *"feeling"* learning. To clarify, right now, imagine yourself inside an inescapable cage with two-inch steel bars. Imagine yourself inside your body looking out through your eyes and really experiencing being in this cage.

As you look at the steel bars, your thinking brain knows immediately that, barehanded, you can't even scratch two-inch steel bars. However, if you focus on your feelings, you will likely notice that your drill sergeant still wants to escape and wants to pound yourself against the bars. You may also notice feeling angry and energized to kick and shake the bars. Your feeling brain doesn't know what your thinking brain knows.

If you imagine kicking and pounding and wrenching at the bars long enough, you will likely experience the emotional part of you tiring, giving up, and letting go with a sigh and possibly a curse word. This sigh signals the emotional learning and letting go.

To enhance your emotional learning and letting go, imagine a recent situation in which you endured self-driving. Picture yourself inside your body looking out through your eyes.

Feel yourself insisting that you fix, change, or accomplish. Let yourself feel interested in getting to know your own demanding side. Don't push or try. Trying usually stimulates unconscious resistance and locks you up. Like an effortless daydream, visualize yourself in a demanding, insisting mood. Notice the physical feeling of tension or pressuring in your body and wait for the misery, frustration, and exhaustion to build. Then hold both the demanding and the distressing feelings until your self-driving system makes the simple but crucial, automatic emotional learning connection between its pressure and the resulting misery.

Continue holding both feelings until they make your drill sergeant sigh, let go, and say, "Oh no, this is painful and exhausting, and it's not working. It's hopeless. I'm going to let go and accept whatever success I can reach." Imagine yourself turning toward your healthy non-pressuring eagerness to succeed and then feeling liberated and energized as you accept whatever large or small success it can carry you to. Because it will—your natural desire to succeed will invigorate you without the debilitating pressure of the drill sergeant, much in the same way a child draws pictures just for the fun of it.

The visualizations in this chapter will help you let your drill sergeant effortlessly emerge and then help you to experience the shudder-producing feeling that it will make you miserable, ruin your day, and may even eventually kill you, whether it's by heart attack or stress-related disease. This will give your drill sergeant a chance to watch over your shoulder, so to speak, as you discover him. Then he or she will gradually become aware of himself or herself wanting to drive you to succeed or fix something. Your drill sergeant feels that if he drives you hard enough, you will succeed. The visualizations gradually let him make the simple emotional connection that his driving doesn't bring success; instead, it brings failure, frustration, exhaustion, and misery.

The visualizations will then guide you to see and feel yourself letting go and turning away as you feel how much you want to turn toward your comfortable healthy motivation.

Wait for your drill sergeant to accept that this healthier motivation, this less serious, effortless eagerness is the only desirable choice. Let that feeling sink in.

What a relief that is. Assimilate this feeling until your body instinctively cringes at the first instance of demand and automatically wants to turn away from it toward the relaxed setting and its comfortable motivation. Most important, recognize that it is not your intelligent understanding of this whole concept that gets your drill sergeant to stop. It is your drill sergeant experiencing the exhaustion and hopelessness that causes it to stop.

Notice that you're not giving up on your dreams. You still want a solution, but you're learning to accept that driving yourself to hurry, worry, and struggle won't bring you success. This acceptance is not limited to your conscious thinking brain that is the focus of traditional therapies. The demanding part of your feeling brain, the source of the problem, is deeply accepting and letting go.

One of my clients, a successful middle-aged entrepreneur, said, "This letting go feels like giving up. I'm not the kind of guy who ever gives up." When I invited him to visualize his drill sergeant trying to make him smash through a stone wall ten feet thick and ten feet high, he easily felt his drill sergeant (which he later described as monstrous) smashing him against the wall. After several minutes he felt exhausted but uttered, "I think I felt it budge that time." He then laughed at his own irrational, unrelenting persistence. Many people feel that if they give up on breaking down the stone wall, they will sit around wasting their lives. This isn't giving up. It's allowing your healthy motivating system to generate an eager, energizing desire to produce or succeed.

Like most of us, you may fear that if you stop driving yourself, you won't succeed. Drill Sergeant Self-Driving is like a giant fireball inside you evaporating your normal healthy desires and exhausting your energies. But what it doesn't realize is that you instinctively enjoy and naturally seek success, ingenuity, creativity, and problem-solving.

Richard Feynman, a physicist who helped develop the atomic bomb, later taught at Cornell and felt burned out from the stress of trying to do excellent and important work. For several years he felt like he was failing and felt depressed and guilty, even though his superiors thought he was doing fine. One day, he remembered when he had once enjoyed physics and decided, "Now that I am burned out and I'll never accomplish anything ... I'm just going to play with physics, whenever I want to, without worrying about any importance whatsoever."

Within a week he was in the cafeteria and noticed a student throwing a plate in the air for fun. He found himself fascinated by the way the plate wobbled as it rotated and wondered about the ratio of wobbling to rotating. When one of his colleagues asked him what was the importance of investigating this, he said, "There's no importance whatsoever. I'm just doing it for the fun of it." Feynman said, "It was effortless. It was easy to play with these things. It was like uncorking a bottle: Everything flowed out effortlessly ... the whole business that I got the Nobel Prize for came from that piddling around with the wobbling plate."

Your natural desire to create and achieve is much more effective than you think. It is more than enough to make you willing to work long and hard. While probably not as intensely serious or gripping as your drill sergeant, healthy desire provides plenty of energy and motivation and is flexible enough to allow your ingenuity, intelligence, and creativity to find unique solutions—a way around the stone wall rather than through it. It isn't as big and powerful as your drill sergeant, but it is ever more enjoyable and effective, and it won't burn you out or ruin your life.

Pushing Yourself Spurs You to Rebel and Fail

One of my clients, a salesman making about $150,000 per year, hadn't filled out his expense reports for over a year. As a result, his company owed him $15,000 and his corporate card was maxed out. He had charged his business travel expenses on his personal credit cards which were also now maxed out. Because his wife had lost her job almost a year earlier, he was heavily indebted and behind on numerous payments. He was stressed out and ashamed that his procrastination and disorganization were so bad that not even his desperate financial straits motivated him to recover his money. He could not understand why he would not fill out these reports, calling himself lazy, stupid, and crazy. He blamed his ADHD and felt that he was damaged and incompetent. Expense reports were due at the end of every quarter and the corporation's books were closed a month or two later. It was possible that he would never recover about $10,000 of his expenses. Yet he still procrastinated.

I explained that it was much more likely that he was rebelling against his drill sergeant by refusing to do his expense reports. The visualizations in this chapter helped him recognize his drill sergeant and teach it to stop pushing him. To get him to experience his healthy motivation without drill sergeant pressure, I invited him to consider a casual experiment in which after work on the coming Friday he would sit at his desk in his home office and not pressure himself to do anything. He would then focus his attention only on his healthy motivation system that wanted his expense money back. I invited him to say to himself, in a delightfully greedy way, "I really want my money." Then I suggested that he look closely at his emotions. If he felt no drill sergeant pressure and only that he eagerly wanted to spend a mere 10 minutes beginning one week's expense report, he could do so. He returned the following week delighted with the fact that when he wasn't pushing himself, he stopped resisting and had enjoyed eagerly "wanting his money back" so much that he had done all 12 expense reports for the most recent quarter.

We all resist pressure, even the slightest implied pressure. Research shows that if you tell people they have to eat a whole bowl of ice cream, they will eat less of the ice cream than if you tell them to eat as much or as little as they want. Forcing yourself to perform stimulates what I believe is a resistance system in your brain to rebel. For example, a business consultant came to see me because he hated himself for achieving only minimal success and for spending most of his free time as a couch potato watching TV. He didn't find TV particularly enjoyable, and he couldn't understand why he watched TV instead of working on the books he wanted to write. He felt that he was a loser, wasting his life. He felt frustrated, depressed, and hopeless.

His drill sergeant system hurled vicious criticism at him in order to force him to succeed as a consultant. He felt inadequate and thought he lacked confidence. It took several sessions for him to fully recognize how intensely he resented and unconsciously resisted his drill sergeant's pressure. For example, he procrastinated, felt too tired to work, and couldn't get himself off the sofa. He daydreamed while he was trying to work. He had a million ways to drag his feet in order to resist being pushed. He secretly enjoyed thumbing his nose at his drill sergeant. When he let go of his destructive demanding, he stopped rebelling and was much more successful.

After several months of considerable success letting go of his destructive demands for achievement and increasing his performance and productivity, the consultant commented that he had lost twenty-five pounds. However, because he had made no progress in the last two months, he was angry and self-critical. He said, "I have no control. It's like an obsession. I can't stop myself anymore. Even if I'm not hungry, I will stand in front of the refrigerator and want to empty it."

To further explore these self-critical emotions, I asked him to imagine standing in front of his refrigerator and to focus on the feelings in his body. I asked him to describe whatever thoughts, pictures, or feelings that came to mind. He said, "I have a feeling in my chest that the chains are off. I'm excited, happy: 'Let's eat!' It's a relief covered by a self-critical, demanding feeling that I shouldn't eat. But eating and drinking are my only real joys. They're a refuge from the rest of my miserable life."

I asked if he could feel the part of him that felt uncontrollable. He said no, and immediately changed the subject. I said that his demands to lose weight may have ignited his resistance system to rebel.

Avoiding these feelings, he responded, "I desperately need to lose weight!"

I said, "That's absolutely logical and reasonable. Unfortunately, your resistance system is in the emotional part of your brain and can't understand logic or reason. If you make it mad, it's unconquerable."

"Unconquerable resistance? I wish!" he replied. "I've always been a wimp. I admired the kids who had the strength to openly rebel and take the punishment from their parents or teachers. I would be red-faced enraged and cursing them, but behind their backs."

I said, "It appears that your emotional system just injected feelings of being weak and frustrated to control and contain your anger and volcanic rebelliousness. This is the same indomitable rebellious system that secretly resists by relentlessly demanding to eat."

He changed the subject again, saying, "Indomitable—baloney. I can't even lose a few pounds!"

I said, "That's the third time your suppressive system has turned your attention away from recognizing and respecting the incredible intensity of your rebelliousness. You need to show it pictures and feelings that will make it feel safe enough to allow you to recognize your intense resistance."

I asked him to imagine feeling certain that even though he might feel strong rebelliousness, by far his strongest desire was to keep his life on the tracks by acting sensibly. His suppressive system gradually became comfortable with his volcanic rebelliousness and let him feel it consciously. He was able to feel that his resistance system would pay any price not to be pushed.

We discussed how losing weight and accomplishing his other goals depended on clearly feeling the immense strength of his unconquerable rebellious side and its determination that no one would force him to diet. Demeaning himself for eating prevented him from recognizing the enormous strength and energy of his rebelliousness. He could succeed only by stopping his misleading self-criticism and, instead, respecting his resistance system. This would allow a working relationship with his rebellious side. For example, he might approach his resistance system with a cooperative feeling such as "I understand you hate being pushed, and I would like to be thinner. What can we work out that would feel acceptable to both of us?"

You Unconsciously Rebel Against Yourself

Resistance (or "psychological reactance" in experimental psychology lingo) is a universal human trait. One of my clients was in chronic pain, and the physician that she liked and respected had prescribed a new medicine that was working wonderfully.

She said, "As I waited in the doctor's office, I was praying he would keep me on this medicine.

"When he said, 'This medicine seems to be working. Keep taking it,' I could not believe it, but I argued with him. Why did I argue with him?"

The rebellious system in our emotional brain helps us maintain our rank in the pecking order or social hierarchy by reacting against any type of demand or pressure. It doesn't know what our thinking brain understands or what other parts of our emotional system desire. It vigilantly watches for pressure, demands, or other actions that would put us in a submissive position and reacts against them regardless. My client's physician took an appropriately dominant position, and her rebellious system instinctively reacted against his dominance.

You pressure yourself and unconsciously fight against this pressure, often undermining yourself and destroying your dreams. This is a minor problem for some and the difference between failure and success for many. Most people want to push themselves hard to develop self-confidence and can't consciously recognize the hidden ways they resist by wasting time or failing to concentrate. Not recognizing how hard your drill sergeant may be pushing you to get more confidence is one of the most frequent obstacles to progress.

To uncover your core confidence, you may first *try* to relax your suppressive system. Often this feeling of trying is actually your drill sergeant pushing you. You won't usually feel this consciously, because your suppressive system has covered it, as it controls other emotions that it might feel are too "hot" or dangerous. Even worse, this pushing stimulates hidden (i.e. suppressed) rebelliousness that locks you in a struggle fraught with confusion and frustration.

For example, the business consultant said, "I'm having trouble getting myself to make time for these visualization exercises, and when I do, I can't concentrate. I have real trouble with procrastination." I told him that procrastination was an imaginary concept that people used when they couldn't see the feelings (usually suppressed rebelliousness) that actually caused them to resist being pressured to act promptly.

"We need to get in touch with whatever feelings are so strong that they are preventing you from using these exercises to uncover the confidence you want," I said. Then I asked him to imagine himself thinking about doing a visualization exercise and to describe the feelings in his body.

"My chest is tense," he said.

I asked him to describe the tight feeling in his chest.

"It feels like someone is pressing my heart really hard." He pushed on his chest with three fingers.

I asked, "What words, images, or thoughts are running through your mind?"

"I'm trying to get myself to do this," he answered.

"It seems that you're pushing yourself."

He said, "I don't feel like I'm pushing myself. I'm setting reasonable goals. I just can't seem to accomplish them."

I said, "Pushing on your chest feels different than asking, 'What would excite you and make you want to do this?'"

I told him he couldn't consciously feel his drill sergeant because his suppressive system was hiding its intense aggressiveness. But his rebellious system could feel his drill sergeant pushing and demanding, so it secretly dug in its heels, refusing to do anything. I urged him to get in touch with both the demanding and resisting feelings in his body. "Feel the tightness in your chest and see if any words come to mind to express that tension."

After a few moments, he said, "You should be doing a lot more. Hurry up!" I then asked him to focus on the tightness in his chest again and let words or pictures that might express a rebellious feeling pop into his mind. After a few moments, he energetically and rebelliously said, "No way!" quickly followed by, "After I felt that rebelliousness, I relaxed and realized that I secretly enjoyed resisting."

He then asked, "Can I make my drill sergeant stop?"

"No. You can't make your lungs stop, either. Yet, once you can feel the gargantuan driving and resisting inside, you will instinctively seek a new approach to this rebellious you. You will appreciate and accept that your rebellious side is never going to give. You will feel, 'I can either stay in this death struggle and fail, or I can respect the rebellious me, stop pushing, and work with it.'"

The more clearly my client could consciously feel his drill sergeant pushing, the more he was able to get that part of himself to become aware of itself and its harsh demanding. As a result, his drill sergeant gradually "learned" that his pushing didn't bring the expected success. Instead it caused rebelliousness, frustration, exhaustion, and hopelessness. Clearly, experiencing the exhaustion and hopelessness made his drill sergeant feel, "This isn't working, and I'm making myself miserable. I've got to stop." Then his drill sergeant let go and stopped. My client made good progress at this process and experienced much-needed relief.

Visualization Will Stop Your Drill Sergeant

Once you've uncovered your drill sergeant, you understand that you need to let go of your destructive demanding, yet it's hard to grasp that your drill sergeant (in the non-thinking feeling brain) won't know what your thinking brain knows. It isn't smart enough to stop because you tell it to. It needs simple pictures and feelings, as in daydreams, to help it clearly feel that its pushing will make you miserable and ruin much of your life. Your drill sergeant can become self-aware and see itself pushing by watching as you clearly picture and feel it demanding and generating its misery. Visualizations work better if you hold the clearest and most sensual image of an insistent feeling until you feel frustration, exhaustion, and hopelessness in your body.

One of my clients, Larry, clearly understood his drill sergeant and that he needed pictures and feelings that would show it that its criticism hurt. Unfortunately, he struggled for weeks to get in touch with his demanding emotions. As a model to follow, I expressed a former feeling that I shared earlier in this chapter in which my own drill sergeant demanded that I perfect a seminar until it would mesmerize audiences. Recognizing his own similar feeling, he hit upon the image that described his drill sergeant: "My drill sergeant is like a pit bull inside me, clamping down and not letting go. He's bred to never stop. He isn't going to listen to what I think or say. I can see and feel him biting down and shaking me. Oh, it's miserable."

Like all of my clients, in these beginning stages, Larry thought that he was feeling or "being" the drill sergeant. However, his statement, "I can see and feel him biting down and shaking me," shows that he was experiencing being bitten and shaken. He was feeling victimized. He was not experiencing his drill sergeant enjoying powerfully discharging its strength and determination to drive him. His conscious feeling was one of misery, of being painfully driven. As I mentioned earlier, his suppressive system, like most, was uncomfortable with his drill sergeant's harsh aggressiveness and magnified his feeling of being driven or victimized to cover up and control his drill sergeant.

When we are fully in touch with our drill sergeant, we can feel how much it enjoys the power, dominance, and pleasure of pushing us (or, in this client's image, biting and shaking). This image often stuns, offends, or even alarms clients. Yet you need to connect with your drill sergeant so that you can actually feel it wanting to drive you. When you are able to feel how much and how harshly your drill sergeant likes to drive you, you are feeling it fully.

Larry said, "It's weird when you talk about enjoying these mean feelings. When you call them pleasurable, that's absolutely nonsensical to me."

I said, "Remember, your drill sergeant was designed by evolution to help you survive. We eat, drink, have sex, and do most other behaviors because they gratify desires; they give us pleasure. Your drill sergeant is part of the same system. It acts because doing so stimulates pleasure systems just like other instinctive processes. Remember your brain has many different systems that function at once. You can walk, talk, and hear all at the same time because different systems control these behaviors. Part of your emotional system can enjoy eating ice cream while another part of your emotional system hates the TV program that your mate is watching. Similarly, your drill sergeant can feel pleasure when discharging its role to drive you to produce or succeed. And simultaneously, other emotional systems can generate a feeling of being driven. I believe that your suppressive system can magnify the feeling of being driven to hide the harsh feeling of driving yourself.

We need to get your suppressive system to let you feel completely comfortable with these aggressive feelings that are instinctively pleasurable. They don't erase your other kinder, more sensible feelings. As you let your drill sergeant's demanding feelings come up inside you, you soon may be able to recognize that it feels pleasure as it tries to drive you to succeed or produce. At first people are often uncomfortable recognizing that their drill sergeant enjoys driving them. But this is a signal that you have allowed powerful self-driving feelings to emerge into consciousness. One way to conceptualize the incredibly complicated brain functions of this emotional learning that then automatically occurs is to think of your drill sergeant as watching you study it. Imagine that as it repeatedly watches you being aware of it, your drill sergeant gradually recognizes itself or becomes self-aware. "It's me demanding!" Once it gains this awareness of itself, it can then in its primitive emotional learning way, connect its driving with the resulting sense of failure, fatigue, frustration, and hopelessness. Then it will stop."

The more fascinated Larry became with his pit-bull insistence, the more he wanted to study it and experience it more clearly. He was able to recognize that his drill sergeant felt pleasure as it drove him powerfully even as it distracted and exhausted other parts of his body. His drill sergeant finally connected its demands to the suffering it created and realized that its demanding would never bring success, only exhaustion and failure, and it stopped pushing. He pictured himself accepting whatever success his normal healthy motivation would bring. Greatly relieved, he began to see his work as being just like his play, something he did for pleasure. He liked making money and helping his clients and found himself eager to do both.

One of my clients, an accountant, gained tremendous relief from a lifelong drill sergeant that forced her to obsessively strive for perfection in her work and personal life. After only a few months of doing the exercises, she stopped making lists every day and no longer worried about mistakes and problems. She said, "It's amazing how much you can get done when you're not fighting a drill sergeant. I feel eager to work instead of tired and frustrated, and I move right along, almost whistling while I work, with no tension or bad feelings."

Smiling, she added, "I've read countless self-help books. And when you first described this strange drill sergeant concept, I wasn't sure that it wasn't just your imaginary friend. Your description of my drill sergeant's strength and intensity made me nervous."

During several weeks of visualizing her drill sergeant feelings using the exercise below, my client uncovered her self-driving feelings and gradually became aware of deeper and more intense levels of them. While visualizing, an image of a giant piston ceaselessly pounding her popped into her mind.

Clients who look at their insistent core and teach it to stop enjoy the most satisfying improvements I have seen in my thirty years as a psychologist. They relish their work, their free time, and their families and friends. That is my wish for you.

Getting Your Drill Sergeant to Let Go

The visualization in the following section will take you through three simple steps. First, we'll reassure your suppressive system that it's safe to uncover your drill sergeant. Second, we'll help you get more deeply in touch with how strong and sensual the demanding critical you is so that your drill sergeant can watch and see what it's actually doing. And third, we'll hold these images until you and your drill sergeant can see that its pushing and criticism bring so much fatigue, frustration, and failure that it decides to stop.

To get this harsh master to stop driving you, look beneath the feeling that you've got to be more or do more. Then you can see and feel your drill sergeant demanding that you perform or achieve. Once you clearly feel the drill sergeant as part of you driving yourself, this emotional part of you will gradually recognize that its merciless pounding, its relentless, primitive demand that you succeed or solve problems brings only misery, failure, and hopelessness. When you watch and feel your drill sergeant pushing you, it's like holding a mirror to your self-driving system so that it can watch with you and see itself pushing and causing you misery. You're helping it become aware of itself.

You're waiting for it to experience the feelings that my 70-year-old client John's drill sergeant recognized, "Oh, this is me. I'm the one demanding. I've been pushing a long, long time, and it's never worked. I cause misery every time I demand, but I don't want to stop. I want to keep pushing, but I can't stand the misery." Once John's drill sergeant finally let go emotionally and stopped pushing, accepting whatever level of success his healthy motivation system would produce, after more than half a century, John finally felt truly free from his drill sergeant's pressure.

Your drill sergeant will shame, threaten, criticize, humiliate, or drive you until you drop. Many people think, "But I don't notice such cruel feelings." Often we can't consciously feel that we are driving ourselves because these harsh feelings are so extreme that they alarm our suppressive system, and it pushes them out of our conscious minds, most frequently by making us feel how we are being pushed, stressed, or frustrated. I call this "feeling the victim side."

To clearly experience your self-driving feelings, we must make your suppressive system more comfortable with your drill sergeant using the same techniques we employed to make your suppressive system comfortable with core confidence.

Visualization to Reassure Your Suppressive System

Close your eyes and imagine that you're inside your body looking out through your eyes and that your reason, kindness, compassion, and commonsense reside in the right side of your body.

Imagine two paths stretching out in front of you. The path to the right is the common-sense-and-compassion action path, along which are good, healthy, sensible, productive actions that keep your life on the tracks. These include treating yourself with respect and kindness.

Can you feel that this path attracts you, that your compassion and common sense want you to choose these healthy actions? These images and feelings of how strongly you're drawn to act sensibly reassure your suppressive system that it's perfectly safe to imagine your more aggressive survival instincts, specifically your drill sergeant, on the left side of your body.

Keeping this feeling that you most want to act sensibly, imagine on the left side of your body your drill sergeant with its demanding feelings to make you fix, produce, or achieve.

Imagine the action path on the left stretching out in front of your drill sergeant. Along this path are the aggressive, demanding actions that your drill sergeant wants you to make, such as hurrying, worrying, making exhaustive lists, and working long hours.

Imagine yourself at a choice point between the two paths. Can you feel your emotional system automatically leaning away from the left-hand insistence? Do both your thinking and feeling brain instinctively lean toward the sensible, right-hand path, strongly preferring what will bring the greatest long-term gain?

Can you feel your emotional system wanting to take the pleasant, productive common-sense-and-compassion action path?

Feeling how strongly you want to keep your actions sensible and productive will let your suppressive system get a good, long look at how safe it is to uncover your demanding, drill-sergeant side.

So, keeping this safe feeling as the atmosphere surrounding you, is it safe to look back over your shoulder to the left and feel your self-critical, destructive demands that you change, improve, or accomplish?

Even if you uncovered your harshest drive to push, rush, or criticize yourself, wouldn't you still feel intellectually and emotionally committed to avoiding these harsh, self-destructive actions and, instead, acting sensibly? When you experience your drill sergeant, you feel its surprising strength. Your suppressive system will have stopped making you feel victimized to cover the drill sergeant's demands and dictates.

Suppressive systems usually require repeated reassurance, and in the beginning there often isn't any noticeable effect. The more you show it these pictures and feelings, the more it will relax and let you see deeper, more intense levels of the pushy, critical side of you. Once you can feel the demanding you, you can teach it that it will never succeed and that it must stop and let go.

Drill Sergeant Visualization

As your suppressive system becomes more comfortable, it will gradually let you experience drill-sergeant feelings and actions that include progressively more intense physical sensations in your body.

When most people begin this process, they can't experience *being* the drill sergeant. They can only feel being driven by it. As mentioned, I call this "feeling the victim side." If you are at this point, you need to spend more time reassuring your suppressive system.

The four main levels of drill sergeant visualizations—from mildest to most intense—are as follows:

1. Imagining someone else's demanding drill sergeant across the room.
2. Picturing yourself across the room being your drill sergeant and pressuring you.
3. Visualizing what it feels like for another person to be inside their body experiencing the drill sergeant's feelings, pushing and demanding, *being* the drill sergeant. (Some may find level three easier to visualize than level two.)
4. Imagining yourself actually inside your body looking out through your eyes and experiencing *being* your drill sergeant driving you.

Keeping a feeling of certainty that your strongest desire is to act sensibly, let's invite your drill sergeant to emerge by imagining yourself in a recent situation in which you were feeling tense or anxious. Perhaps you were struggling to complete a task or achieve a goal that you didn't have enough time, control, or information to accomplish. Begin at the level with which you are comfortable. See if you can picture level 4 by imagining yourself inside your body looking out through your eyes as if you're actually in the stressful setting now, experiencing your stress, feeling "the victim side." (If it's too intense, imagine seeing yourself across the room. A little distancing is okay.)

You might focus by saying to yourself, "Whatever hidden, self-driving feeling that is creating this stress is perfectly safe to feel clearly."

Is your strongest desire to act sensibly? Of course! So it's okay to let the drill sergeant appear.

Wait for your suppressive system to relax and let your drill instructor surface more fully. It usually appears first with words or thoughts such as "Accomplish something!" or "Right this wrong!" or "Fix this NOW!" or "Hurry up!" or "You shouldn't have made those mistakes!" or "You should've already been successful!" or "You're nothing until you're great!" Some people begin without words and feel only a vague physical sense of their drill sergeant's pressure or urgency pushing them to be smarter or better or hurrying them to do more, faster.

Many people fear experiencing these harsh feelings, but most of us have them. The more clearly you see your drill sergeant's intense emotions, the better you can deal with them. When you're finally really in touch with them, you'll feel strong and empowered, yet clear headed and easily able to act sensibly.

To get even more in touch with the strength of your inner drill sergeant, look closely at how it expresses itself in your body. You may have an urge to clench your fists, grind your teeth, tense your stomach, or pound your heel against the ground.

To get a better look at your aggressive, demanding feelings, release them into one or more of these physical expressions or movements. For example, clench your hands or jaws. Experience the physical sensations of driving yourself. This physical exercise helps you identify with the deeper aggressiveness of your hidden drill sergeant. Experience the demanding part of you. Feel the driver. Be the driver.

How much difference is there between your drill sergeant's negative, critical demanding and healthy, positive encouragement?

Do you understand that your drill sergeant feels entitled to push you? It was sculpted by evolution to enjoy pushing you forward, driving you to succeed or survive. It's completely natural to feel these pressures. There was a time when your drill sergeant's insistence was necessary, a time when you needed to persist in finding water or killing dinner, but that time is past now. You don't need this drill sergeant now, today.

Does the confusion, frustration, and misery caused by your drill sergeant prevent you from thinking clearly, feeling confident, acting decisively, and getting things done? Can you feel that positive encouraging motivation would help you perform better?

Notice also that your drill sergeant's demands may stimulate your resistance system to rebel, saying, "Nobody pushes me!" Occasionally this rebelliousness is conscious and easy to recognize in thoughts or statements such as "I don't like being pushed," or "You can kiss my fanny," or "I'm not going to do it!" Usually, this resistance is hidden deep inside, and we see only the results of our rebellion in confusion, fatigue, forgetting, hesitation, or procrastination. In this exercise, we're waiting for your drill sergeant to realize it's causing the painful symptoms of rebelliousness.

Don't push. Be patient. Let your interest in your drill sergeant's strength and destructiveness effortlessly rivet your attention on its demanding feelings. The more fully you let it emerge the more you will feel and respect its inborn desire to drive you to success.

Focus on your drill sergeant until you feel the frustration, failure, and exhaustion it creates. (This usually takes fewer than ten minutes.) Hold the demanding feeling until your slow-learning drill sergeant finally connects its demanding with the misery and exhaustion that it causes. Wait for your drill sergeant to grasp that it has only two choices: suffer frustrating rebelliousness and continue to fail miserably; or stop, let go, and accept what you can and can't do.

When it says, "Oh, this is me demanding. I've done this a lot, and it has never helped. It always hurts. My demanding will never work," then you've gotten through. Enjoy letting go.

It's hard for us to wait long enough for this learning to occur, because we're used to consciously making things happen the instant we want them to happen. We can't make this happen any faster than it will naturally. We're waiting for your drill sergeant to make a feeling, non-thinking connection— to achieve a self-awareness that pushing and criticizing will never work. We're waiting until it says, "I want to keep pushing, I was born to push, but if I do, I'll be tense and miserable forever, and I'll create so much rebel-liousness that I'll never have any success. I might as well stop." The more you experience these cruel, self-driving feelings, the more your drill sergeant becomes self-aware, realizing, "Oh yeah, I am making me miserable. I can't stand this. It's not working. I'm never going to get what I want. I don't want this pain anymore!"

It's crucial that you're not just *thinking* this. You and your drill sergeant must make this connection at the emotional level. We don't know if that will require a day, a week, or a month. However long it takes, it's worth it. Life is so much easier when your drill sergeant stops driving you.

Your tension and anxiety are not usually created by a third party, a situation, or even your own personal limitations, but by your drill sergeant. It's not that you desperately need to succeed, speak well, fix something, go to sleep, get a raise, or make life better. It's your drill sergeant mindlessly insisting, pushing.

While many people attribute their success to pushing themselves hard, they could have accomplished much more if they had not stressed themselves with ruthless, unrelenting demands. My clients have felt that if they give up and let go, they'll end up mediocre or they'll sit around wasting their lives. They don't, and you won't. The healthy, undemanding part of you wants to fix problems and enjoy success. Once you stop pushing and accept that you can't finish every list or make every deadline, you can relax and enjoy what you actually can accomplish.

Your drill sergeant believes that if it doesn't drive you, you'll have no motivation and you'll fail. It has no respect for your healthy motivating system that wants to enjoy the instinctive pleasure of fixing, achieving, or producing. Drill sergeants usually consider this system ineffective. At this point, show your drill sergeant a clear picture of healthy positive motivation making you eager to perform or succeed.

Keep these feelings prominent in your mind so that your drill sergeant can watch them mobilizing you.

Once your demanding feelings subside, embrace your healthy eagerness to enjoy success. Visualize yourself veering away from the path of pushing and criticizing and stepping into a situation in which you relax and enjoy performing naturally, effortlessly, and powerfully. Recognize that the healthy you wants to enjoy success and will sweep you toward it enthusiastically.

Now, here's the hard part: Wait for your drill sergeant to let go and accept what your healthy motivation can actually accomplish. This isn't the perfect success your drill sergeant demands, but it's still satisfying because your natural eagerness for success carries you forward effortlessly. The only chance you have to comfortably succeed is to stop pushing and let your natural desire for success lift you.

References

Brehm, J. W. (1966). *A theory of psychological reactance*. New York: Academic Press.

Brehm, S. S., & Brehm, J. W. (1981). *Psychological reactance*. New York: Academic Press.

Feynman, R. P., & Leighton, R. (1985). *Surely you're joking, Mr. Feynman!* New York: W. W. Norton.

CHAPTER 9

Additional Confidence-Releasing Techniques

I've got enough confidence in myself to believe that when I'm healthy and hitting my shots, no one can beat me. Great athletes have to think like that."
— JULIUS "DR. J." IRVING, NBA FORWARD

As I stated earlier in this book, people learn via modeling. You can sharpen your awareness of raw confidence by watching exceptionally confident people. Watch Oprah Winfrey do anything, watch Bette Midler sing, or watch videos of Michael Jordan in slow motion (especially Michael Jordan's *Come Fly with Me*). Relax, open your mind, and watch their body language. Even if you can't release your core confidence yet, you can get a feel for it. Videos of great speakers, such as Winston Churchill, Franklin Roosevelt, John Kennedy, and Dr. Martin Luther King, Jr. also provide superb models of core confidence.

Movies, television, and theater provide excellent models of people pleasurably and successfully channeling core confidence. It's fun watching these characters, partly because we enjoy seeing them express the confidence we ourselves unconsciously want to release. Rhett Butler, the character played by Clark Gable in *Gone with the Wind,* is the classic, confident male. Focus on his demeanor and body language until your feeling brain clearly recognizes core confidence. The following movies present actors portraying remarkably confident characters:

- *Gone with the Wind*—Clark Gable and Vivien Leigh
- *Boom Town*—Spencer Tracy and Clark Gable
- *Casablanca*—Humphrey Bogart and Claude Raines
- *To Have and Have Not*—Humphrey Bogart and Lauren Bacall
- *Shane*—Alan Ladd
- *Funny Girl*—Barbra Streisand
- *The Man Who Would Be King*—Sean Connery and Michael Caine
- *The Color Purple*—Oprah Winfrey
- *The Thomas Crown Affair*—Steve McQueen
- *Patton*—George C. Scott
- *Silence of the Lambs*—Anthony Hopkins
- *The Fugitive*—Tommy Lee Jones
- *A Man for All Seasons*—Paul Scofield
- *Catch Me If You Can*—Leonardo DiCaprio
- *The Godfather*—Marlon Brando
- *Gladiator*—Russell Crowe
- *True Lies*—Arnold Schwarzenegger
- *The Matrix*—Keanu Reeves
- *True Grit*—John Wayne and Kim Darby
- *American Beauty*—Kevin Spacey

Two of my favorite models are William Shatner as Denny Crane and James Spader as Alan Shore on the TV sitcom *Boston Legal.*

Photo Modeling

Select photographs of individuals who embody the poise that you wish to release. Magazines such as *Time* and *People* have high-quality photos. Place these photos where you will see them often and enjoy visualizing yourself exuding similar confidence. Your suppressive system will warm up to the raw confidence with each subsequent exposure.

The Core Confidence Game

Goal: See who can exude the most core confidence.

Get together with a friend or friends for a confidence contest in which you compete to exude the most confidence in the wildest statement. Grade not only the content, but also give style points for the depth and genuineness of the feeling. Humor naturally softens the intensity of raw confidence, making it less threatening to your suppressive system. For example, open the contest by asking, "Who's going to come in second?" Then proclaim, "I am the world's greatest _____. All bow when I enter." Try these hot but harmless feelings of core confidence in a fun and friendly atmosphere. Have fun and show your suppressive system how safe, energizing, and mind clearing your core confidence is.

Core Confidence Greeting Contract

Arrange with a friend that each time you talk, you will begin by letting some core confidence roll out in a grand statement. Adding humor, especially at the beginning, allows you to try on confident feelings with less threat to your suppressive system. For example, say, "I'm so much cooler than you!" This exercise shows your suppressive system that these hot feelings are harmless. The more comfortable you become, the more intense confidence you can release. Then you won't need the humor.

I Am the Greatest Exercise

After you have made substantial progress through the earlier exercises, this advanced exercise helps you safely release delightful core confidence. It will help you feel and understand your core confidence and your secret struggle to repress it.

Stand up, so that you can release your emotions more fully.

Put your arms at your sides and visualize pleasurable, confident feelings in your body. You can picture them as electricity or as a white light if you like.

Visualize yourself effortlessly discharging your biological belief in yourself as you throw your arms up in the air and yell, "I am the greatest!"

Were you able to fully release or did you notice holding back? Are you suppressing your confidence with criticism? Remember, these exercises may determine how much confidence you have for the rest of your days.

If you are having trouble letting go, visualize yourself letting go safely and pleasurably.

Enjoy this exercise several more times and do some harmlessness checks as described in Chapter Six. Notice that your confidence increases each time you release more fully.

Unleash Your Confidence! A Master Plan

Recognize core confidence as a legitimate part of your personality and the source of your belief in yourself. Remember, there's no harm in a feeling. So frequently, while eating, showering, or waiting in line, visualize yourself feeling a raw primordial confidence along with a clear awareness that you can still easily decide to act appropriately and unpretentiously. These visualizations will gradually relax your suppressive system and let it begin releasing more confidence.

The next time your palms sweat or you feel insecure, open your mind to what hidden core confidence might be stimulating your suppressive system to needlessly create these painful, paralyzing feelings. If some primitive word, image, or thought comes to mind, recognize it as a clue.

Notice and respect any signs of your core confidence. For example, if you have a cocky feeling such as "I'm so much better than she is," don't criticize it. You won't start acting conceited simply because you feel core confidence. A cocky feeling will not erase your wisdom, manners, or compassion for others. It will make you feel good about yourself.

Each step in the following master plan will help you frequently bathe your suppressive system with desensitizing images and messages.

1. Keep resources, such as this book and the other recommended readings, visible as an invitation to explore and harness your hidden confidence. *Play with a concept from this book each day.*

2. If you have friends who would be open to these ideas, discuss them. Suggest that your friends take the Confidence Suppression Test. Comparing scores will make for lively, desensitizing discussion. Ask them about their own core confidence. Watch them as they suppress their confidence by denying, avoiding, or changing the subject. Notice how suppression limits your friends.

3. Respect raw confidence and notice that it's universal. Even those who deny feeling core confidence often indirectly demonstrate it. Notice how your dog thinks you should be petting it instead of another dog or the cat or instead of doing anything else. Watch children profess that they can do things they can't. Notice your family members and friends feeling that they cook the best, look the best, or tell stories the best. How many people feel their opinion is the best? Accept that we all biologically feel our child, parent, sibling, team, or country is the best.

4. Be patient and persistent. Notice small gains in calmness, poise, or assertiveness and feel encouraged by them.

5. Regularly retake the Confidence Suppression Test and the Baseline Confidence Measure in Chapter 2 to feel encouraged about your progress.

6. Each time you catch yourself suppressing your confidence, you are making progress.

7. Regularly review sections in this book and revisit the exercises.

8. Persist. I have seen clients plagued with world-class suppressive systems persist for a year with little progress, and then finally feel major releases of delightful core confidence. It's worth it!

Recommended Reading

Books can't catch your suppressive system in the act of undermining your confidence, but the following books (listed in order of helpfulness) will deepen your understanding of your core confidence. As mentioned earlier, the books by Wright, Buss, and de Waal provide an important summary of the new and interesting field of evolutionary psychology. Those by Simon, de Camp, Zweig, and Bly provide additional information that will familiarize you with the primitive instincts that exist inside all of us.

- Robert Wright, *The Moral Animal*
- David Buss, *The Evolution of Desire*
- Frans de Waal, *Our Inner Ape*
- Robert I. Simon, M.D., *Bad Men Do What Good Men Dream*
- L. Sprague de Camp, *The Ape-Man Within*
- Connie Zweig and Jeremiah Abrams, *Meeting the Shadow*
- Robert Bly, *The Human Shadow*
- Robert Bly, *A Little Book on the Human Shadow*

Discover Suppressed Confidence in Your Thoughts and Feelings

1. Frequently write down whatever confident feelings and fantasies come to mind.
2. Write without criticizing what you have written. Ignore grammar, mechanics, or any other formal rules.
3. After you finish, or even days later, reread what you have written to identify any suppressive feelings, such as depression, helplessness, or inadequacy. Recognize them as suppressive tools and notice what comes to mind about the primitive confidence they may be hiding. Open your mind to see if any clues or symbols of your underlying core confidence pop up.
4. Reassure your suppressive system by recalling images and feelings of how easily you have controlled your actions in the past.
5. Do this as often as it is enjoyable and interesting.

The Confidence List

This exercise will help you recognize, respect, and remember the primitive confidence and suppressive emotions that you encounter. Play with it every day. Record (or at least think about) the raw confidence you have felt or have seen someone express today. Examples are provided to stimulate your memory. Write down the who, what, and where of the circumstances. Remember that your emotional brain responds to pictures, so capture vivid details that make the scene memorable and real to you.

Confidence Experienced Today

I felt or saw someone else feeling raw confidence.

Circumstances:

Feelings Used as Suppressive Tools Today

Did I feel anxious, afraid, guilty, helpless, hopeless, depressed, power-less, abused, or victimized in order to suppress my confidence? If so, did I open my mind to words, thoughts, or images that might indicate the underlying suppressed core confidence?

Specifics:

References

Bly, R. (1988). *A little book on the human shadow.* San Francisco: Harper & Row.

Buss, D. (1994). *The evolution of desire.* New York: Basic Books.

De Waal, F. (2005). Our inner ape. New York: Riverhead Books.

Ferguson, H. (1983). *The edge.* Cleveland: Getting the Edge Company.

Simon, R. (1996). *Bad men do what good men dream: A forensic psychiatrist illuminates the darker side of human behavior.* Washington, DC: American Psychiatric Association.

Wright, R. (1994). *The moral animal.* New York: Random House.

Zweig, C., & Abrams, J. (1991). *Meeting the shadow.* Los Angeles: Jeremy P. Tarcher.

CHAPTER **10**

Conclusion

"Whatever you can do or dream you can, begin it. Boldness has genius, power and magic in it."

— JOHANN WOLFGANG VON GOETHE

This is not a time to struggle with your failures and shortcomings. This is a time to look deep inside yourself, down through your fear and self-doubt, all the way down to your biological core. This is a time to let your raw belief in yourself rise up and fill every cell of your being with an exhilarating certainty that you can do anything, that you're magic.

Doubt, failure, and disaster don't exist for your core confidence. No matter how impossible the situation, this primitive instinct expects triumph. It doesn't understand how much smarter, stronger, or more experienced your competitors are. It not only doesn't remember your shortcomings, it never saw them in the first place. And it won't ever see them. It follows one program only: to make you feel that you're unbeatable and deserve to be at the top of the pecking order.

Core confidence is truly the sun rising within you, driving out pessimistic gloom and breathing into you the poise, passion, and optimism to bring all your power to bear on your challenges, win or lose. You think clearly, plan carefully, and act courageously. And if you fail, it makes you eager to rise and charge again. Core confidence can deliver us from cataclysm and give us, individually and collectively, our best life and our best chance at greatness.

Whether or not you can actually become president, hit a home run, or discover a cure for cancer, *feeling* that you can lets you perform at your best and relish every moment of being alive.

For half a century, I've been at war with the hidden juggernaut that crushes our biological belief in ourselves. This book gives you the tools to claim your birthright: your bottomless belief in your own worth, strength, and talent. You don't have to build it or heal it. Just stop being afraid of it. At stake for you or your loved ones is the chance to live fully, laugh loudly, and reach for your dreams.

At stake for us collectively is unimaginably more. Our world is foundering in a sea of debt, war, weather disasters, and political gridlock. Running scared or hunkering down won't save us. Core confidence will excite and empower us with the feeling that we're smart enough and strong enough to meet any challenge.

Everything—success, happiness, concentration, and determination—flows from this wellspring of feeling that you're worthy, that you can do anything. Most people who make major contributions to humankind are swept forward by a deep belief in themselves. Find your sense of greatness and let it excite and empower you to make your own contributions. Once you see yourself in a new way, it's a new world. You see your friends, family, and others in a new way.

Somewhere inside you, you already believe in yourself. Look deep and keep looking and keep soaking in reassurance. Believing in yourself is living; everything else is just existing!

Stay in Touch

I'd like to know if you begin to believe in yourself and if you uncover confidence beyond measure, and any other comments or criticisms that you have. You can email me at BernardSullivanPhD@gmail.com.

If you'd like to work with me personally, visit www.ConfidenceBeyondMeasure.com or email me. Coaching sessions will be available individually or in groups, both in person or by phone. Separate groups will be available for salespeople, coaches, athletes, performers, students, parents, public speakers, therapists, managers and executives, and those interested in assertiveness or dating and personal relationships.

There will be other resources at www.ConfidenceBeyondMeasure.com. These will include a blog, troubleshooting information, and a chat room for you to ask questions and share experiences. I recorded audio versions of visualization exercises that will be available for download or on CD.

References

Ariely, Dan. (2008). *Predictably irrational.* New York: Harper Collins.

Bandura, A., & Walters, R. (1963). *Social learning and personality development.* New York: Holt, Rhinehart, and Winston.

Barkley, R. (2011). Executive functioning: Impairments and treatment. http:// www.caddac.ca/cms/video/teens_adults_player.html.

Bly, R. (1988). *A little book on the human shadow.* San Francisco: Harper & Row.

Bly, R. (1990). *Iron John.* Reading, MA: Addison-Wesley.

Brehm, J. W. (1966). *A theory of psychological reactance.* New York: Academic Press.

Brehm, S. S., & Brehm, J. W. (1981). *Psychological reactance.* New York: Academic Press.

Buss, D. (1994). *The evolution of desire.* New York: Basic Books.

Clark, R. (1971). *Einstein: The life and times.* New York: HarperCollins.

de Camp, L. (1995). *The ape man within.* Amherst, MA: Prometheus Books.

Denney, D. R., Sullivan, B. J., & Thiry, M. R. (1977). Participant modeling and self-verbalization training in the reduction of spider fears. *Journal of Behavior Therapy and Experimental Psychiatry, 8,* 247-53.

Denney, D. R., & Sullivan, B. J. (1976). Desensitization and modeling treatment of spider fears using two types of scenes. *Journal of Consulting and Clinical Psychology, 44,* 573-79.

De Waal, F. (2005). Our inner ape. New York: Riverhead Books.

Dillon, M., Minchoff, B., & Baker, K. (1985-86). Positive emotional states and enhancement of the immune system. *International Journal of Psychiatry in Medicine, 15,* 13-17.

Emerson, R. (1904). *The conduct of life.* Boston: Houghton Mifflin & Co.

Ferguson, H. (1983). *The edge.* Cleveland: Getting the Edge Company.

Feynman, R. P., & Leighton, R. (1985). *"Surely You're Joking, Mr. Feynman!": Adventures of a curious character.* New York: W. W. Norton.

Garfield, C. (1984). *Peak performance*. New York: Warner Books.

Gawain, S. (1978). *Creative visualization*. San Rafael, CA: Whatever Publishing.

Gilbert, M. (1994). *In search of Churchill: A historian's journey*. London: Harper Collins.

Greenwald, A. (1992). New look 3: Unconscious cognition reclaimed. *American Psychologist, 47,* 766-79.

Gregory, S. W., and Webster, S. (1996). "A nonverbal signal in voices of interview partners effectively predicts communication accommodation and social status perceptions." *Journal of Personality and Social Psychology,* 70, 1231-1240.

Gregory, S. W., and Gallagher, T. J. (2002). "Spectral analysis of candidates' nonverbal vocal communication: predicting US presidential election outcomes." *Social Psychology Quarterly,* 65, 298-308.

Krugel, M. (1994). *Jordan: The man, his words, his life*. New York: St. Martin's Press.

Leno, J. (2004). *The actors studio* [Television broadcast]. New York: Bravo.

Loftus, E., & Klinger, M. (1992). Is the unconscious smart or dumb? *American Psychologist, 47,* 761-65.

Maltz, M. (1960). *Psycho-cybernetics*. New York: Prentice Hall.

Manchester, W. (1983). *The last lion: William Spencer Churchill*. Boston: Little, Brown & Co.

Peale, N. (1956). *The power of positive thinking*. New York: Prentice-Hall Press.

Pribram, K. H. (1962). Interrelations of psychology and the neurological disciplines. In Koch, S. (Ed.), *Psychology: a study of a science*. New York: McGraw-Hill.

Remnick, D. (1998). *King of the world*. New York: Random House.

Simon, R. (1996). *Bad men do what good men dream: A forensic psychiatrist illuminates the darker side of human behavior*. Washington, DC: American Psychiatric Press.

Sharot, T. (2011). *The optimism bias*. New York: Pantheon Books. Pg. xv.

Sperling, D. (1989). *Michael Jordan: Come fly with me*. New York: NBA Entertainment.

Sullenberger III, C. (2009, January 15). *60 minutes* [Television Broadcast]. New York: CBS.

Sullivan, B. J., & Denney, D. R. (1977). Expectancy and phobic level effects upon desensitization. *Journal of Consulting and Clinical Psychology,* 45, 763-71.

Trivers, R. (2000). The elements of a scientific theory of self-deception. *Annals NY Acad Sciences* 907:114-31.

Trivers, R. (2009). Deceit and self-deception. In: Kappeler, P., & Silk, J. (Eds.) *Mind the Gap* Berlin: Springer-Verlag.

Twenge, J., & Campbell, W. (2009). *The narcissism epidemic*. New York: Free Press.

Whitaker, M. (1998). *Michael Jordan unauthorized: A collection of quotes in four quarters*. Chicago: Bonus Books.

Williamson, M. (1992). *A return to love*. New York: Harper Collins

Wood, J., Perunovic, W., & Lee, J. (2009). Positive self statements: Power for some, peril for others. *Psychological Science, 20,* 860-66.

Wrangham, R. (1991). Is military incompetence adaptive? *Evolution and Human Behavior, 20,* (1): 3-17.

Wright, L. (1995, August 7). Double mystery: Recent research into the nature of twins. *New Yorker Magazine,* 45-62.

Wright, R. (1994). *The moral animal*. New York: Random House.

Zweig, C., & Abrams, J. (1991). *Meeting the shadow*. Los Angeles: Jeremy P. Tarcher.

About the Author

D r. Sullivan received his Ph.D. in psychology from the University of Kansas in 1977. He has been in private practice in counseling, executive coaching, and sales training for 34 years. He has been studying self-confidence for 50 years. In 1986, he founded the country's first psychology/self-improvement store: The Creative Mind, which offered 5,000 books, tapes, and videos.

Dr. Sullivan has presented seminars for businesses and professional organizations, such as AT&T and The American Business Women's Association. He has published three articles in major psychology journals. He is a member of the American Psychological Association, the Kansas and Missouri Psychological Associations, and he is listed in the National Register of Psychologists. He has received three awards from the Kansas Association of Professional Psychologists. A former Golden Gloves boxing champion, he lives with his wife in a suburb of Kansas City.